D1269769

GREECE BEFORE HOMER
ANCIENT CHRONOLOGY AND MYTHOLOGY

GENERAL EDITOR
WILFRID J. MILLINGTON SYNGE

GREECE
BEFORE HOMER

ANCIENT CHRONOLOGY AND
MYTHOLOGY

Sir Edgar JOHN FORSDYKE
K.C.B.

Prisca fides facto sed fama perennis

MAX PARRISH · LONDON

MAX PARRISH AND CO LTD
55 QUEEN ANNE STREET LONDON W I
FIRST PUBLISHED 1956

PRINTED IN GREAT BRITAIN
BY FLETCHER AND SON LTD NORWICH AND
THE LEIGHTON-STRAKER BOOKBINDING CO LTD LONDON

CONTENTS

ILLUSTRATIONS
IN HALF-TONE

PREFACE

In writing this introduction to the archaeological and literary records of prehistoric Greece, I have had in mind readers who may not be prepared for critical consideration of these matters as presented in books which quote ancient authors in their original languages and refer to international academic publications. I have therefore omitted footnotes and have cited the Greek authorities in translation.

The purpose of the book is to explore the processes by which prehistoric narratives were adopted in historical Greek literature and elaborated with realistic details of genealogy and chronology. The archaeological documents are authentic records of the times that they represent, but they do not explain themselves. The literary statements are explicit, but unauthentic in the sense that they were not contemporary with the events that they describe. Such testimonies cannot legitimately be used to explain archaeological discoveries unless they are themselves supported by external evidence.

I have transcribed Greek words with no more change than English *c* and *y* for *k* and *u*, except in names which are familiar in English or Latin forms, as Plutarch and Aeschylus. This apparent inconsistency has the advantage of distinguishing between literary works which we possess, and those that exist in fragments or not at all. Thus Apollodorus is the author of the well-known mythological *Library*, Apollodoros of the lost *Chronography*.

HOMER

Conjectural dates for Homer – the Epic Cycle – Photius and Proclos – author-ship of 'Iliad' and 'Odyssey' – personality and name of Homer – epic origins – Bronze and Iron Ages – Homeric references to iron – burial and cremation – the Muses – introduction of writing – oral tradition – ancient editions of Homer – the Homeridai – interpolation – historical content.

The conjecture of Herodotus, that Homer lived not more than four hundred years before his own time, that is to say in the last half of the ninth century B.C., is likely to be as near the truth as any. Other ancient estimates ranged from the twelfth to the seventh century. Modern speculation has covered the same extent of time, or more, and has formulated other problems which were not perceptible in antiquity. The two questions of Homer's relation to the *Iliad* and *Odyssey*, and of their narratives to historical fact, have become remarkable for extreme expressions of contradictory opinions. At one end a single poet is said to have composed these records of his own age which have survived without considerable alteration, at the other the two poems were a growth of centuries in the repertories of professional reciters trained in a traditional style. The persons represented were real Greeks and Asiatics who attacked or defended the city of Troy at a certain moment in history, or reflections of Achaian chiefs engaged in tribal warfare at distant times and places in Greece. The problems exist, but their solutions are more likely to be found in less arbitrary interpretations of probabilities and possibilities.

The question of the poet's date is rather literary than historical. The historical significance of the *Iliad* and *Odyssey* lies in their subject-matter, which belongs mainly to the Heroic Age of Greece before the coming of the Dorians, the last and most destructive of the intrusions of northern tribes which reformed the nation as Herodotus knew it.

There was a large body of heroic poetry, similar in kind but various in quality, some of which was ultimately arranged in narrative sequence as the Epic Cycle. This put together the whole story of the prehistoric Greek world from the creation of the gods to the end of the generation that knew the Trojan War. The last poems of the series, which may be called the Trojan Cycle, were eight in number, in order of events the *Cypria, Iliad, Aithiopis, Little Iliad, Sack of Troy, Returns, Odyssey,* and *Telegony.* We owe our knowledge of the composition of the Epic Cycle to Photius, the industrious Patriarch at Constantinople in the ninth century.

Photius was a scholar whose other talents engaged him in the vicissitudes of political and ecclesiastical life. He was twice appointed Patriarch and died in exile, but his literary work was continuous and permanent. He presided at meetings of a literary society at which works of ancient and modern authors were read and criticised. Before leaving Constantinople on a diplomatic mission to people whom he called Assyrians (meaning one or more of the Moslem powers of Western Asia) he dictated for his brother Tarasios a digest of two hundred and eighty volumes which had been read when the brother was not present.

Among the books thus recorded was an abridged version of a handbook of classical Greek literature, the *Chrestomathia* of one Proclos. Photius says of it:

Read extracts from the Literary Chrestomathy of Proclos. [Here follows a description of the book.] He deals with what is called the Epic Cycle, which begins with the mythical union of Sky and Earth (and their monstrous progeny), and continues with other mythological tales of the Greeks about the gods and some that may contain historical truth. The Epic Cycle, compiled from various poets, ends with the landing of Odysseus in Ithaca, where he was also killed unwittingly by his son Telegonos. He says that the poems of the Epic Cycle are preserved and generally studied not so much for their merit as for the narrative of events that they contain. He also gives the names and places of origin of the poets represented in the Epic Cycle.

The author of the *Chrestomathia* was identified by Suidas with the Proclos of Lycia who was head of the Neoplatonist School at Athens in the fifth century A.D. Whoever he was, it is evident that the poems of the Cycle were extant in his time, but had been lost (with the exception of the *Iliad* and *Odyssey*) before the time of Photius, doubtless as a result of the closing of the pagan schools by edict of the Emperor Justinian in the year 529.

The book that Photius read was an abridged copy of Proclos. Brief summaries of contents of the six lost poems of the Trojan Cycle, which are prefixed to the tenth-century *Codex Venetus* of the *Iliad*, are fragments of the same book.

In the time of Herodotus, and even later, much more than the *Iliad* and *Odyssey* was popularly attributed to Homer, notably the *Cypria* and the two epics of the Theban War, *Thebaïs* and *Epigonoi*, as well as the *Hymns* which are still called Homeric. All these poems seem really to have been anonymous, but later Greeks did not like anonymity, and when literary experience recognised as the work of Homer no more than the *Iliad* and *Odyssey*, possible authors had to be provided for the rest. The latest poet thus admitted to the Cycle was Eugamon of Cyrene, to whom some attributed the *Telegony*, in the sixth century; others placed it in the seventh century as the work of Cinaithon of Sparta. The *Telegony* related the adventures of Odysseus after the killing of the suitors, his death at the hand of Telegonos, Circe's son, who had come to Ithaca in search of his father and had been mistaken for a pirate, and the happy marriages of Telegonos with Penelope and Telemachos with Circe. These sentimental developments and the peaceful succession of Orestes to the kingdoms of Argos and Lacedaimon marked the end of the Heroic Age. The Dorian Invasion, which later Greeks regarded as the beginning of their real history, was placed in the time of Orestes' son Tisamenos.

The *Iliad* and *Odyssey* are manifestly older than the other epics of the Trojan Cycle, which were composed as introductions or sequels to them. Their unique survival, by a natural process of selection from the whole epic body, attests their superiority in other respects. It was perhaps an unmerited misfortune for some of the poets of the Cycle that the word 'cyclic' also meant commonplace or conventional, but it was justly applied in that sense to the recurrent themes and diction of the post-Homeric epics. Some poems of the Cycle seem to have had considerable merit. Pausanias says that the *Thebaïs*, which many competent critics regarded as the work of Homer, was in his opinion the next best after the *Iliad* and *Odyssey*. But so far as can be seen in the summaries of Proclos and the few quotations that survive, the other poets of the Trojan Cycle lacked the dignity and dramatic power of Homer, and their poems did not have the artistic unity of the *Iliad* and *Odyssey*. That they were later in time is apparent in their enlargements of the legend with new geographical knowledge and genealogical invention.

A few Alexandrian scholars went so far as to ascribe the *Iliad* alone to Homer, but they had no following in later antiquity. It was however suggested as a compromise that the *Iliad* was the work of Homer's maturity, the *Odyssey* of his garrulous old age. Most modern critics have assigned the *Odyssey* to a different and later author. Apart from formal similarities of style and diction, which they shared with all the epics of the Cycle, the *Iliad* and *Odyssey* resemble each other in their dramatic design, in delicate portrayal of character, and in the expression of a serene and sensitive humanity which is strangely mated with the brutalities of the battlefield in the *Iliad*. The original design implies a single author in each case; the power of characterisation can belong to many, as to the Attic dramatists; but the rare humanity is the reflection of the poet's character, and might be decisive for single authorship if it could be taken by itself. Factual differences in the *Odyssey*, a fuller consciousness of the poet's own world, can be explained by the different theme: there was less traditional material and more room for invention in the personal experiences of Odysseus. A more mature vocabulary and other linguistic variations may point to a later date and another author. But it must be borne in mind that we do not possess the original text of either poem, and the *Odyssey* seems to have been more heavily interpolated than the *Iliad*. Allusions to the final scenes at Troy and the post-war adventures of other heroes may have been introduced by later editors to create authority for the Cyclic sequels. It can only be said now that if the *Iliad* was not composed by the same poet as the *Odyssey*, it was certainly the model on which the *Odyssey* was formed.

Nothing was known about the person who was called Homer, beyond the fact established by the epic dialect, that he belonged to an Aiolic or Ionian city; but many mythical biographies supplied the want of traditional information. The people of Smyrna said he was the son of their river Meles, and that his real name was Melesigenes (Child of Song). Others, with an eye to chronology, made him a descendant of Orpheus in eleven generations, and a cousin of Hesiod, Orpheus being a son of the Muse Calliopê. Others again made Calliopê the mother of Homer. A more realistic school of genealogists, gathering inside information from the *Odyssey*, made him the son of Phemios, the domestic minstrel of Odysseus, or a son of Telemachos, his mother being a slave-girl sold in Ithaca, like Eumaios, by Phoenicians, or Polycastê, Nestor's youngest daughter who gave Telemachos his bath when he called at Pylos. That, they said, was why Homer spoke so well of Nestor.

The name was not more real than the person. It was said to have been applied to blind people in Aiolic cities; but this was certainly not the meaning of the word. Homer's alleged blindness was adopted from the minstrel Demodocos in the *Odyssey*. A better explanation of the word but not of its use as a name, was that it meant a bond or surety, and that the poet was so called because his father (not Meles or Telemachos) was taken as a hostage from Cyprus by the Persians. The sense of the word in epic use was fellowship or company, and it is easy to see how that preceded its classical meaning of hostage. The Muses of the *Theogony* sing in company with one another (*homêreusai*); a messenger accompanied the swineherd of the *Odyssey* on his way to the city (*homêrêse*). Common cognate forms in classical Greek were *homílos*, a crowd, and *homília*, an assembly or a discourse (homily) delivered to companions.

The original epos, before the use of writing, was necessarily preserved by fraternities of poets or reciters who would have held their repertories in common and could hardly recognise individual authorship. The fact that the Cyclic poems were at first anonymous, then classed together as the works of Homer, and long afterwards distributed among more or less fictitious authors, implies that Homer was not a personal name, but may have been a general term for the members of a poetical corporation (*Homêroi*). It can thus be used legitimately for the poet from whom, directly or indirectly, the *Iliad* and *Odyssey* received their form and character.

The language of the poems is colonial, and the Trojan background is put in with experience acquired in Asia, but the Achaian heroes are domiciled in European Greece at a time before the social and political upheaval caused by the coming of the Dorians. It seems certain that the emigrant princes who led the Aiolic and Ionian colonists took with them the Court minstrelsy that had belonged to their families in Greece. Phemios and the blind Demodocos entertain the assembled companies in the palaces of Ithaca and Scheria with tales of the Trojan War. Achilles appears at Troy as his own minstrel, singing deeds of glory to himself. These original lays are represented as being partly mythological but mainly historical. Homer's achievement was to create from some of them the great dramatic unity of the *Iliad*. Others would have supplied material that was used in the *Odyssey* and by the poets of the Cycle and the school of Hesiod.

The period represented in the epics was the end of the Bronze Age. Homer certainly lived after the final establishment of the Greek colonies in Asia, at a time when bronze had long gone out of use for edge-tools and weapons, and he could not have had personal knowledge of an age when men habitually drove to battle in chariots instead of riding horses, fought with bronze-bladed swords and spears, and carried large leathern shields on shoulder-straps. Nor could he have invented the details of these prehistoric realities which are established now by archaeological discovery. He must have reproduced them from earlier poems which were contemporary with the events that they described. By doing so he established the heroic conventions which were preserved, together with the archaic diction, throughout the life of the Greek epic and in its Alexandrian revival.

Material differences between the world of Homer and that of his poetical sources were easily recognised. Hesiod defines the conditions of the Bronze Age explicitly: 'Zeus made the third generation of mortal men, a brazen race. Their weapons were of bronze, their houses of bronze, and they worked with bronze: there was no black iron.' It was also understood on the historical side that Dorians must not be mentioned. But the *Iliad* and *Odyssey* record other prehistoric peculiarities which would have been less perceptible to the poet and hardly at all to his audiences, in tribal organisation, law and custom, social and domestic life, religious practices and supernatural beliefs.

In face of Hesiod's definition of the Bronze Age, all Homeric references to iron would seem to be anachronisms. But it is worth while to examine them in detail, noting first that Hesiod placed the Age of Heroes between the generations of bronze and iron. That antiquarian observation on the part of the poet can only mean that iron was often mentioned in the epics. There are twenty-three separate references to it in the *Iliad*, nineteen in the *Odyssey*, and they fall into several groups. Most of them are in metaphorical contexts: Achilles, Priam and Penelope are iron-hearted on occasion, Odysseus will not be kept away from home even by bonds of iron, fire has iron strength, a man's flesh has not, an iron noise goes up to the brazen sky, or the sky itself is iron. Telemachos says, proverbially, 'iron draws a man' when he puts the (bronze) weapons out of reach of the quarrelsome suitors. Fabulous strength is the idea in the iron gates of Tartaros and the axletree of Hera's chariot, and a famous iron club, a reminiscence of Nestor's childhood, seems to belong to this group. The term may be used in a generic sense for blades or points in the iron of the arrow with which Pandaros wounds Menelaos, and the iron that slaughtered oxen feel in their throats.

All these references are anachronistic in relation to the subject-matter of the poems. They reveal familiar experience of iron, and may come from Homer or his successors or his immediate predecessors. Arrowheads, being an expendable munition of war, would be among the last things to be made of iron: in historical times they were usually cast in bronze. This is the only weapon that is said to be made of iron, but some iron tools are mentioned: the knife with which Achilles may cut his throat, and several axes, including the famous series through which Odysseus shoots the arrow.

The last and most interesting group of references may belong to the original epos. Iron in these is a valuable commodity: part of the conventional wealth of a rich man; one of the attractive products (with gold, bronze and women) of sacked cities; raw metal shipped from the Adriatic coast to Cyprus in exchange for bronze, or given by Achilles as a prize at the funeral games of Patroclos. Achilles explains that this particular mass will be useful to the winner for making agricultural implements. His statement, and the fact that some knives and axes in the poems, but no actual weapons, are made of iron, agree with some historical indications that the first use of iron by expert bronze-workers was not for military purposes. Its tempering for effective swords or spearheads seems to have been a difficult process, but short or heavy blades could be produced for knives and axes.

The iron swords with which the Celtic tribes met the Roman legions in their invasion of Italy in the third century B.C. are described as being of very poor quality. Polybius says of them:

Their swords had no points and could only deliver one effective downstroke, which at once put them out of action, the blade being so much bent and twisted that unless the wielder had time to rest it on the ground and straighten it with his foot, it was useless for a second blow.

The moment in metallurgical development indicated by the last group of Homeric references would be the transition from the Bronze to the Iron Age, and the probability that some of these came from the original epos is supported by a more definite cultural element in the poems, the funeral rite of cremation. It is the only rite described in the *Iliad* and *Odyssey*, but in all the periods and regions of the full Greek Bronze Age, Thessalian, Helladic, Cycladic, Minoan and Mycenean, the dead were simply buried or perhaps preserved in some way in built tombs. In historical times they were buried with or without burning. Cremation must therefore have been introduced at the very end of the Bronze Age, and archaeological evidence indicates that it was accompanied by the first use of iron.

Accurate observance of the life and manners of the distant past is a phenomenon peculiar to the early Greek epic. It is noticeably absent from the French heroic poems, although these came nearest to the Greek in their historical conditions. The rapid contamination of the legend of Charlemagne was doubtless due in large measure to its transmission in a literate society. Reading and writing hasten the process of imitation, and as Plato says in the *Phaedrus*, destroy memory: not the mechanical memorisation of the rhapsode, which Socrates derides in the *Ion*, but the knowledge acquired through the discipline of oral instruction. But some stronger force than professional schooling or antiquarian interest must have compelled Homer and his predecessors to preserve the poetical traditions so faithfully. That was doubtless the religious sanction of the Muses, daughters of Zeus and Memory.

The early Greek poet passed as an inspired prophet of the Muses; on the human side his art seems to have been an inheritance, as Elisha received the mantle of Elijah. Homer was said to have given the manuscript of the *Cypria* to Stasinos of Cyprus as his daughter's dowry, that of the *Oichalia* to Creophylos of Samos as a friendly gift. In later times the divine inspiration became a form-

ula or a pretence, but its original reality is seen in the invocation
which precedes the Catalogue of Ships in the *Iliad*:
Tell me now, ye Muses who dwell on Olympus, for you are
goddesses and are present and know all things while we hear only
rumour and know nothing: tell me who were the leaders of the
Danaoi and their captains.

In the Hesiodic and Cyclic poets reverence is giving way to in-
sincerity. 'Tell me, O Muse,' says the poet of the *Little Iliad*, 'of
things that never happened before and will never happen again.'
The Muses of the *Theogony* tell of 'Things that were and are and
will be'; and in his strange prelude the poet makes them say: 'We
know how to utter falsehoods that seem like truth, but we know
how to tell the truth when we want to'. That cynical admission
is the kind of thing one might have expected from an early Ionian
philosopher, Xenophanes or Heracleitos, who said that Homer
and Hesiod ought to be thrashed for their obscene theology.
The sweet-voiced Hesiodic Muses have in fact transferred their
patronage from the historical content of poetry to its artistic
form: 'From them and from Apollo it is that there are poets and
musicians upon earth.'

The comparatively safe transmission of the original epos can
thus be attributed to strict oral discipline supported by divine
authority. The primitive Muses were formidable deities: the mythical Thamyris lost his eyesight by setting up in opposition to them.
Homer evidently stood at the end of a long poetical tradition, for
the elaborate hexameter verse was certainly not new to him. He
did not put inherited poems together in a continuous narrative,
but adapted them to a single dramatic design. This apparently
miraculous birth of Greek poetry in mature literary form, like
Athena springing from the head of Zeus, can only be explained
by the sudden operation of an external agency, in this case the
introduction of writing.

The earliest inscription in the Greek alphabet that has yet been
found is cut on the body of a small pottery jug which is painted
in the Geometric style of Athens (Plate 1). The jug was evidently

offered as a prize at some festivity, and the inscription reads, in hexameter verse: 'He whose performance is best among all the dancers shall have me.' The chronology of Geometric vase-painting is not satisfactorily established, and this piece has been placed at various points between the middle of the eighth century and the beginning of the seventh. The first inscription that can be securely dated is cut on the leg of a statue of Rameses II at Abu Simbel above the First Cataract of the Nile. It is a short list of names of Ionian soldiers employed by the Pharaoh Psametik II on a Nubian expedition at the beginning of the sixth century. The wide difference in time between these two documents has aroused some doubt as to the relation of the first inscription to the vessel on which it is cut; it might of course be a late addition, although an old jug of that modest quality would hardly have been an attractive gift. But other finds of pottery at Athens and Corinth in recent years have established the facts that the inscription was contemporary with the jug, and that the jug should be dated about the end of the eighth century.

Among some thousands of early potsherds excavated from the site of a sanctuary on Mount Hymettos at Athens there are thirty-one which bear more or less fragmentary inscriptions. These belong to formulas of dedication or imprecation: one identifies the deity of the sanctuary as the goddess Earth (*Gaê*), another bears the name of a person Nicodemos, who was apparently consigned to perdition with the opprobrious epithet *catapygon* (sodomite). The Greek alphabet is represented here in its mature form. Some of the inscribed pieces are painted in the Geometric style but are later in date than the jug with the complete inscription, and should be placed at the beginning of the seventh century.

These documents attest the popular use of writing at Athens and its application in correct orthography to colloquial speech and trivial occasions before the end of the eighth century. Allowance must be made for its general diffusion before that time, and still more for the production of the Greek system, which was not, in the developed form presented here, a mere adoption of Phoenician letters. The vowels were differentiated, and signs for some consonantal sounds, which the Semitic languages did not possess, were added at the end of the alphabet.

The alphabetic script doubtless had its origin in commercial relations of Ionian and Phoenician traders; its adaptation to Greek language and literature is likely to have been the work of priestly or professional bodies such as the colleges or guilds by whom the oral tradition of poetry was conveyed. A system which met with general acceptance cannot have been produced by isolated individuals or the community at large. The perfected script may also have been held by its producers for some time as hieratic property, a new testament of Apollo or the Muses. The Sumerian art of cuneiform writing was learnt at temples of the gods, and was held by its possessors as 'a secret treasure'.

A hundred years do not seem to be too many for the consecutive processes of professional formation and use, general diffusion in Ionia and oversea, and popular application as it appears on the common pottery of European Greece at the end of the eighth century.

Caesar's note on the Gaulish Druids presents an instructive example of professional reticence in regard to writing:

They are said to learn large quantities of verse by heart, and some of them stay under instruction for twenty years. They think it wrong to transmit this knowledge in writing, although in most other matters for public and private purposes they make use of Greek letters. I think they have established this practice for two reasons: they do not want their instruction to become common knowledge, nor those whom they instruct to rely on writing and neglect memory.

That is not to say that the Druidic colleges had no written texts: a script under proper control secures the oral tradition. 'Large quantities of verse' in detached forms or narrative sequences can be composed and held in memory, but it is unlikely that such long artistic unities as the *Iliad* and *Odyssey* could be constructed without the aid of writing, and likely that these elaborate works were

associated with its introduction. That can hardly be placed later
than the ninth century.

The hieratic use of writing is also represented in Hebrew tradition. When the prophet Isaiah had a political message to deliver,
warning the Judaean government against taking part with Israel
and Syria in resistance to Assyria, he received a divine injunction
to put it into writing. He did so in the presence of two 'faithful
witnesses', Uriah the High Priest and another, who would have
certified that the scribe had made a true record of what Isaiah said.
The document ended with the instruction: 'Bind up the testimony,
seal the message among my disciples': that is to say the disciples
were to keep the roll as their authority and to promulgate the text
by word of mouth.

Three or four generations later, when Damascus and Samaria
had fallen to the Assyrians and Nineveh itself had fallen to the
Medes and Babylonians, Jeremiah was moved to preach sub-
mission to Babylon. His divine instruction was:

Take thee a roll of a book and write therein all the words that I
have spoken to thee against Israel and against Judah and against all
nations, from the day I spoke unto thee, from the days of Josiah
even unto the present day. Then Jeremiah called Baruch the son
of Neraiah, and Baruch wrote from the mouth of Jeremiah all the
words of the Lord which he had spoken unto him, upon a roll of
a book. And Jeremiah commanded Baruch, saying I am shut up, I
cannot go into the house of the Lord. Therefore go thou, and read
in the roll, which thou hast written from my mouth, the words of
the Lord in the ears of the people in the Lord's house upon the
fasting-day.

In the sequel the words came to the ears of the young king, Jehoiakim, who then demanded the roll. When three or four pages had
been read to him, he cut it with a penknife and threw it into the
fire that was burning on the hearth, doubtless believing that by
destroying the text he would destroy the record of the prophesies.
But

Then took Jeremiah another roll and gave it to Baruch the scribe, who wrote therein from the mouth of Jeremiah all the words of the book which Jehoiakim the king of Judah had burned in the fire, and there were added besides unto them many like words, a demonstration of the superior power of memory which would have delighted Socrates, and an instructive illustration of the editorial process of enlargement.

The first ancient notice of the Homeric text was a legend which is recorded by Cicero, Pausanias and others to the effect that the books of Homer, previously detached and dispersed, were assembled and arranged at Athens in the sixth century by direction of Peisistratos. An earlier Greek version of the story said that Hipparchos, the elder son of Peisistratos, was the first to bring the poems to Athens, and had them recited by relays of rhapsodes at the Panathenaic Festivals. Others attributed that ordinance to Solon or vaguely 'to our ancestors'. The underlying facts seem to be that Peisistratos and his sons, like other enlightened rulers of their time, collected literary texts for public use, and that continuous recitation of the *Iliad* was an old institution at the Panathenaia. The inference is that the Athenian authorities produced a standard text for their own use in controlling these official recitations.

There is no reason to doubt that there was an Athenian edition in the sixth century. It would explain the presence of some Attic elements in the language, and certain obvious interpolations tending to the political advantage of Athens at that time. But there is no reason to suppose that it was more than a recension of the text, and the stories imply that its immediate purpose was to eliminate undesirable variants. This edition may also have been published in manuscript; in any case, commercial publication seems to have begun about that time. The texts chosen for collation by Alexandrian scholars were designated by the names of cities, presumably those from which the Ptolemaic Library had bought them, or of individual editors. Marseilles and Sinope are among the five or six places mentioned; an early editor whom the Alexandrians regarded with respect was Antimachos of Colophon, an epic poet of the fifth century.

Commercial or private production might be expected to corrupt the text, but the competitive nature of the book trade, and the suspicious nature of Greek criticism, would discourage editorial exuberance. Herodotus says that Onomacritos, a literary and political associate of the Peisistratids, was expelled from Athens by Hipparchos for inserting verses of his own into the poems of Mousaios.

Some authority must have preserved the text with considerable accuracy between the time of Homer and the institution of civic or commercial control in the sixth or fifth century, and one would expect to find it in Ionia, where five or six cities claimed to be birthplaces of Homer.

There was in Chios an association of persons who called themselves Homeridai (Sons of Homer), and were professionally concerned with public recitations of Homeric poetry. Their constitution and functions are noted in several ancient testimonies. They were said to have been described by the mythographer Acousilaos in the sixth century as a family group in Chios taking their name from the poet. Since Acousilaos was one of the first prose writers, no earlier record could be expected. Pindar, in the fifth century, calls them 'singers of woven lays', with allusion to the supposed origin of the term 'rhapsode'. Plato, in the fourth century, makes the prosperous rhapsode Ion say that he ought to receive a gold crown from the Homeridai for his superlative expositions of Homer. In the *Phaedrus* Plato quotes a hymn to Eros as belonging to the epic archives of the Homeridai.

A scholiast on the passage in Pindar says that they were in the first instance descendants of the poet, who recited his poems by right of inheritance, and were subsequently rhapsodes who did not belong to the family. The associates of one Cinaithos were particularly active members of the guild, and were said to have inserted many of their own compositions into Homer's poetry. Cinaithos was said to have written the *Hymn to Delian Apollo* which Thucydides thought was Homer's. Another scholiast says that the Homeridai committed the poems to memory and published them (orally?) in a fragmentary condition, and did them a lot of damage. Eustathius, commenting on Homer in the twelfth century, says the same thing about Cinaithos and his school, and gives their activities as the reason why the works of Homer had to be corrected. The alleged forgery of Cinaithos is the hymn which ends with the pretended signature of Homer:

> *A blind man who lives in rocky Chios,*
> *Whose songs will all for ever be the best.*

These statements, which are mostly gathered by late writers from earlier sources, may not be accurate in detail, but they offer a satisfactory explanation of the process by which the texts of the early epics were at once preserved and contaminated. The travelling rhapsode might improve his recitation or his script (if he had one), but his improvements could hardly find their way into a current text unless they were accepted by his school. When commercial publication of manuscripts began, the Homeridai and similar bodies would have lost their usefulness and their creative opportunities. When Plato wrote they were probably a literary society which celebrated Homer as its eponymous founder.

Guilds and societies with patronymic titles imitating those of family groups were a regular feature of Greek professional organisation. The greatest and most widely known were the colleges of physicians and surgeons, the Asclepiadai; the Pamphides, who are said by the lexicographer Hesychius to have sung the hymns of Pamphôs at Athens, must have been a very small feminine guild. Asclepios was ultimately a god, whatever he may have been in the first instance, and all the medical practitioners of Greece cannot have believed in their lineal descent from him, although the claim was made, in sixteen generations, on behalf of the great Hippocrates of Cos. Galen honours Asclepios as 'our ancestral god'. Pamphôs was the name given to the reputed author of certain traditional poems which were popularly believed to be older than Homer.

An important hieratic body, the Eumolpidai, took its name from one of the mythical founders of the Mysteries at Eleusis. Attic historians gave Eumolpos many diverse origins, but his name reveals him as a transparent personification of vocal music. In that capacity he was appropriately the son of Mousaios, to whom some ancient Eleusinian hymns were attributed. Otherwise he was a Thracian king (Thrace being the mythical home of the Muses), a son of Poseidon, who assisted the Eleusinians in a war with Athens in the time of Erechtheus or two hundred years later.

In historical times the Eumolpidai were responsible for much more than music at Eleusis. They had general control of the Mysteries, and were particularly concerned with religious discipline. In his speech for the prosecution in a notorious case of impiety at Athens at the end of the fifth century, the orator Lysias appeals to the unwritten laws which were held and interpreted by the Eumolpidai, and of which no man knew the author. They were therefore, like the Homeridai, the custodians of an oral tradition, and were also in a position to take notice of meritorious performance in the ritual. An Athenian epitaph recording their award of a wreath (*eiresionê*) to a small boy, Thesmophanes, apparently for his excellent singing, recalls the crown of gold which Ion of Ephesos did not get from the Homeridai.

It is evident that there are several strata in the composition of the *Iliad* and *Odyssey*. The nucleus, consisting of the original epos, must have been enlarged to some extent during the period of oral transmission, but perhaps not materially altered if professional authority and the sanction of the Muses were effective. The change from a more primitive metre to hexameter verse is to be placed in the course of this time.

The next stratum, which is properly Homeric, contains the many alterations and additions necessary to the new design of the two great poems, particularly the fictitious Trojan element formed upon the Achaian model. Precise delineation of character and circumstantial detail, which gives its vivid reality to the narrative, belongs to Homer's art; the real or pretended knowledge of Asiatic places and persons reflect the interest of Aiolic and Ionic colonists in their new country.

The post-Homeric stratum belongs mainly to the period of Hesiodic and Cyclic poetry, when publication of the epic was still oral but a written text was held and enlarged by poetical authority. Commercial publication of manuscripts, beginning in the fifth century or earlier, would put an end to large-scale interpolation. Small variations or additions by individual editors or publishers did not find general acceptance, and our present text seems to have been well established in the time of Plato. Greek purchasers were discriminating, not to say suspicious, in these matters. The poet Aratus, in the third century B.C., is said to have asked his literary friend Timon how he could get a reliable text of Homer. Timon told him to look out for an old copy and not to buy a revised edition.

Contamination is a relative term in textual criticism. Interpolated passages in Homer are not necessarily inferior in quality; many which cannot be detected now may have been inserted by the guilds or colleges because of their poetical merit. The tenth book of the *Iliad*, the Episode of Dolon, is an addition of this kind, but its later date is marked by differences of language and ideas. Short episodes, such as the famous Exchange of Armour by Glaucos and Diomedes, may have been excerpts from other poems. Other early interpolations are the twenty-fourth books of the *Iliad* and *Odyssey*, both added for the sake of rounding off the stories or connecting them with their Cyclic sequels.

Many explanatory lines may have got into the text by accident, having been marginal comments in the first instance, as the unlikely mention of Aithra's name for one of Helen's handmaids. The notorious line connecting Salamis with Athens in the *Catalogue of Ships* is as obvious as any of these; indeed all the references to Athens in the *Iliad* may be interpolations. If they are, they represent the last successful attempts to manipulate the text, for the *Iliad*, according to Herodotus, was being cited as a national authority in the crisis of the Persian War.

Historical statements in the epics have therefore to be examined critically to determine their probable age or origin. But the *Iliad* and *Odyssey* generally present a consistent and convincing picture of the heroic world, convincing because it is confirmed by evidence which was not within the knowledge of the historical Greeks. The contributions of Homer to history are not so much in events and personalities as in details of domestic and military life and in social and political conditions.

2

GREEK CHRONOGRAPHY

Transmission of ancient chronography – Eratosthenes, Apollodoros and Castor – Eusebius and Jerome –kings of Lacedaimon – generations and regnal years – traditions of Lycourgos – early historical chronology – years of office – Olympiads – the discus of Iphitos – fraud and forgery – prehistoric scripts –legendary relics.

The date that has been generally accepted for the Fall of Troy, 1183 B.C. in modern terms, was established by Eratosthenes of Cyrene, Principal Librarian in the Museum at Alexandria at the end of the third century. He was not a professional historian, but an encyclopaedic scholar who wrote on many subjects, grammar, literature, philosophy, geography, astronomy, mathematics; and he was also a poet. His colleagues called him *Pentathlos* for obvious reasons, and more maliciously, *Beta*, because the all-round athlete was not expected to be first in any single event. His *Chronographia* was a comprehensive and rational system which sought to date events by contemporary evidence. For that reason he began with the Fall of Troy, or rather with the Dorian Invasion, the cardinal point in their history which the Greeks called the Return of the Heracleids. It was accepted as a fact that the Return took place two generations after the Fall of Troy, and the two generations were usually counted as 80 years. The initial date with which Eratosthenes was concerned was therefore 1103, after which, as he thought, some existing records were reliable, or could be made so.

There were several reasons for the success of Eratosthenes' book. It was supported by the reputation of its author and the Library. It satisfied a general need by putting together in convenient form the historical knowledge of his time, and by disposing of the accumulated discrepancies of previous writers. His dates for the earliest periods, where speculation had been most active, were moderately estimated, and were presented as the results of critical research. General acceptance of his conclusions was secured through their adoption by his immediate successors in the field of chronology, Apollodoros of Athens and Castor of Rhodes.

Apollodoros, who wrote mnemonic chronicles in verse, was more popular than Eratosthenes, and more useful because he brought the story down to his own time, 140 B.C. Eratosthenes had stopped at the death of Alexander in 323. Castor, in the first century B.C., compiled a comparative chronology of the world, Oriental, Greek and Roman. In order to establish some equality with the much older Egyptian and Asiatic histories, he carried Greek chronology back to the earliest legendary or imaginary events. Systems of heroic chronology had been elaborated long before by the romantic historians of the sixth and fifth centuries, Hecataios, Hellanicos and others, and Castor probably did no more than reduce their speculations to consistent order, as Eratosthenes had done with the historical records.

Castor's work was largely used in the cosmopolitan scholarship of Roman and Byzantine times, notably by Christian writers who were concerned to bring pagan history and legend into line with Hebrew biblical tradition. The only one of these ecclesiastical chronologers whose work has survived to any considerable extent was Eusebius, Bishop of Caesarea in Palestine in the fourth century. His two books of Chronicles of the World exist mainly in Latin and Armenian translations from the Greek. The first book, the *Chronography* proper, is an historical summary in narrative form with frequent references to and excerpts from classical authorities. The second book was called the *Canons*, because it presents the several chronologies in parallel columns, the years of Egyptian, Asiatic and Greek kings, Olympiads and Roman Emperors being aligned with those of Abraham. The Latin version of the *Canons*, made by Saint Jerome at the end of the fourth century, was the text-book of ancient chronology in medieval

Europe. The Greek chronology of Eusebius was mainly derived from Castor, and Castor's (from the Fall of Troy to the death of Alexander) from Eratosthenes.

Later Greek historians said that Eratosthenes (or Apollodoros) founded his early chronology on the reigns of the kings of Lacedaimon. Those kings were recognised as being direct descendants of the first Dorian conquerors. If authentic records of their names and reigns had existed, there would have been no doubt of the date of the invasion, and Eratosthenes could have done no more than assign uncertain events to certain years of successive kings. But Clement of Alexandria says that he placed the Return of the Heracleids 327 years before the First Olympiad (776 + 327 = 1103 B.C.), and Diodorus, following Apollodoros, says that the length of that interval was computed from the reigns of the Spartan kings. The achievement of Eratosthenes was therefore to bring the Lacedaimonian lists into an acceptable relation with the Olympic era by adjusting the sum of years between the First Olympiad and the Return. Diodorus in this passage gives the interval as 328 years, because in the normal Greek manner he includes both terminal points. Clement was careful to say that it was counted to the year before the Olympiad. This ancient arithmetical ambiguity has led to the variation of a year in some medieval and modern versions of the date, 1184 for the Fall of Troy and 1104 for the Dorian Invasion.

The dual dynasties at Sparta, the Agid and Eurypontid lines as they were called, claimed descent from Heracles through the twin sons of Aristodemos, Eurysthenes and Procles, who were said to have been born at the moment of the Return. The descent from Heracles is manifestly fictitious, the story of the twins has the appearance of a fable derived from the two dynasties, and some of the earlier names in the pedigrees are not above suspicion. Even if the lines had been unbroken through several turbulent centuries and the names had been preserved by oral tradition, the lengths of the reigns could not have been recorded accurately before the use of writing.

Our earliest records of the Lacedaimonian kings are the genealogies attached by Herodotus to the Agid king Leonidas, who was killed at Thermopylai in 480 B.C., and the Eurypontid Leotychides, who commanded the Peloponnesian fleet in the following year.

The pedigrees recorded by Herodotus are collated here with the lists of kings reported six hundred years later by Pausanias and confirmed by earlier authorities.

GENERATIONS	PEDIGREES IN HERODOTUS		SUCCESSION OF KINGS IN PAUSANIAS AND OTHERS	
1	Heracles			
2	Hyllos			
3	Clodaios			
4	Aristomachos			
5	Aristodemos		Aristodemos	
6	Eurysthenes	Procles	Eurysthenes	Procles
7	Agis	Eurypon	Agis	Soös
8	Echestratos	Prytanis	Echestratos	Eurypon
9	Labotas	Polydectes	Labotas	Prytanis
10	Doryssos	Eunomos	Doryssos	Eunomos
11	Agesilaos	Charilaos	Agesilaos	Polydectes
12	Archelaos	Nicandros	Archelaos	Charilaos
13	Teleclos	Theopompos	Teleclos	Nicandros
14	Alcamenes	Anaxandrides	Alcamenes	Theopompos
15	Polydoros	Archidamos	Polydoros	Zeuxidamos
16	Eucrates	Anaxilaos	Eurycrates	Anaxidamos
17	Anaxandros	Leotychides	Anaxandros	Archidamos
18	Eucratides	Hippocratides	Eucrates	Agesicles
19	Leon	Hegesilaos	Leon	Ariston
20	Anaxandrides	Menares	Anaxandrides	Demaratos
21	Leonidas	Leotychides	Cleomenes	Leotychides
			Leonidas	Archidamos

The first kings in these lists whom we can date securely are Anaxandrides and Ariston, who were reigning together, according to Herodotus, when Croesus of Lydia sent envoys to them seeking an alliance against Persia. That would have been shortly before the conquest of Lydia by Cyrus in 546 B.C.

Both lines go back to Heracles in 21 generations. Herodotus says elsewhere that he counts three generations to a century. That would place Heracles at 1180 B.C. But Herodotus also says that Heracles lived 900 years before his own time, and that the Trojan War was little more than 800 years ago. These dates would be about 1340 and 1250 B.C. Herodotus is therefore not giving here his own estimate of time, but is repeating the received opinion of his day, derived perhaps from his predecessor Hecataios of Miletos, who seems to have assessed the generation at 40 years.

Herodotus says that when Hecataios was at Egyptian Thebes he told the priests of Amen that his sixteenth ancestor was a god. His statement did not impress the priests, who showed him that their own ancestry went back eleven and a half thousand years. Sixteen generations at three to a century would place the god 530 years before Hecataios, about 1050 B.C., hardly earlier than the traditional founding of Miletos and too late for divine interference with human pedigrees. A generation of 40 years would put him safely back into the Heroic Age, not far from the time when, according to Herodotus, Penelope became the mother of the god Pan. The two generations between the Fall of Troy and the Return of the Heracleids were usually counted as 80 years on this older estimate.

Discrepancies between the reigns and generations, which begin to appear with the dawn of history, imply that the regular succession from father to son in the earlier series was artificial. It was known, for instance, that the successor of Theopompos (in whose reign Eratosthenes placed the First Olympiad) was his grandson. Leotychides, the last king here in the Eurypontid list, was the first of a collateral line. His descent in eight generations from Theopompos is exhibited in the pedigree of Herodotus, but he is seventh in dynastic succession from Theopompos. He and his Agid colleague Leonidas both came to untimely ends. Leonidas was killed in battle in the tenth or eleventh year of his reign, Leoty-

1 The earliest known inscription in the Greek alphabet, cut on the body of a pottery jug. The painting on the neck is in the Geometric style of Athens.

2 Clay tablet from Mycenae,
incised with Minoan script 'B'
(13th century B.C.).

(*Left*) Clay ball impressed with
Cypriote script (14th or 13th
century B.C.). (*Right*) Bezel of
a gold signet ring engraved with
Minoan script 'A' (from Cnossos; about 1500 B.C.).

chides was found taking bribes in Thessaly in his twenty-second year, and did not go back to Sparta. He was succeeded by his grandson; the predecessor of Leonidas was his brother.

Eponymous ancestors in Greek genealogies are rightly suspect, and it may well be that Agis and Eurypon were persons invented to explain the names of the families, as the twins (who ought to have been the eponyms) had their origin in the unexplained phenomenon of the two dynasties. Several of the Eurypontid kings have names which are more symbolical than personal. Soös was not recognised by Herodotus, and his name (Safe) seems to be related to that of the divine counterparts and patrons of the dual monarchy, the Dioscouroi, who were the Saviour Lords (*Sotêres*) of Laconia. Prytanis (President) and his son Eunomos (Legal) are too aptly political to be true. Both of them were related by various devices to Lycourgos the legislator, whose Spartan constitution was the *Eunomia*. But Herodotus knew Lycourgos as the uncle of Labotas of the other royal house.

There were also doubts as to the relation of the first ancestors to the moment of the Return. Aristodemos, father of the twins, was a vague personality, if not mythical. He was generally said to have died before the entry into the Peloponnese: one story was that he was shot by Apollo at Delphi for by-passing the oracle, another that he was murdered there by the sons of Pylades and Electra. But the Lacedaimonians themselves, 'contradicting all the poets', as Herodotus says, insisted that he led them into Laconia.'

It is evident that if the 16 or 17 generations from Aristodemos or his sons to Leonidas and Leotychides were computed at three to a century, they would give a low date for the Dorian invasion, 1013 or 1046 B.C. against the 1103 of Eratosthenes. But he did not have to deal with generations nor with long lists of kings. Before his time the kings had been provided with regnal years, which were fictitious for the earlier periods and based upon the long generations of Hecataios. The process was to distribute the sum of generations among the number of reigns with a plausible variation of years.

The regnal years of the Agid kings are presented by Eusebius on the authority of Diodorus, who took them from Apollodoros, that is to say, it is the list used by Eratosthenes. It is translated here from the Latin of Saint Jerome:

THE KINGS OF THE LACEDAIMONIANS

Eurysthenes	42 years
Agis	(31)
Echestratus	35
Labotas	37
Doryssus	29
Agesilaos	44
Archelaus	60
Teleclus	40
Alcamenes	37

whose tenth year was Olympiad I.

The current texts assign a single year to Agis, but that would be in itself impossible, in view of the many events attributed to his reign and to his importance as the eponym of the dynasty. The correct number, 31, can safely be restored from the statements of Diodorus and Clement of Alexandria that Eratosthenes allowed 327 (or 328) years between the Return and the First Olympiad. Eusebius copied Diodorus here in counting to the tenth year of Alcamenes; Clement says that Eratosthenes counted to the ninth. Eusebius also says that he equated the tenth year of Alcamenes with that of his Eurypontid colleague Theopompos.

The years of the eight kings placed by Eratosthenes before Alcamenes range from 60 to 29, and their sum is 318, giving an average reign of nearly 40 years, equivalent to the Hecataian generation. But these long reigns and generations are wholly at variance with ordinary probabilities and the analogies of later history. The average length of reigns of historical Spartan kings is 23 years, that of their generations 32. Three generations in a century are in fact a normal measure of life. The regnal years were certainly fictitious, the regular succession of generations improbable, and the lists, which can only have been recorded orally, were evidently defective in other respects. In any case they can have had no value as a measure of time.

Before the adoption of the Olympiads as a chronological canon the historians did not attempt to express their prehistoric dates in precise or absolute terms. Herodotus says that this or that occurred so many hundreds of years before his time, in the case of the Trojan War rather more than eight hundred. Since he was said to have been born in 484 B.C. and lived until the last years of the century, the precise moment that he had in mind, if any, is not determinable. These periods are usually counted from the time at which he may be supposed to have been writing his *History*, about 440 B.C. His eight hundred years for Troy were evidently based upon the eighteen generations from the Lacedaimonian kings of his time, Pleistoanax and Archidamos, to the Return, *plus* two to the Fall of Troy: twenty generations assessed at the old rate of forty years each. If he had applied his own rate of three generations to a century, he would have dated the War at least a hundred years later.

The idea of establishing precision in these matters was a much later development. All the dates for the Trojan War, except those that were sheer guesses, seem to have been derived from the Lacedaimonian lists. There was ample room for variety in different estimates of generations, but the later results were presented as if they were based upon regnal years and Olympiads, to which they had really been adjusted. The junction of the historical Olympiads with the fictitious years of the kings was a point at which several chronographical systems diverged. The Laconian Sosibios, an elder contemporary of Eratosthenes, placed the First Olympiad in the thirty-fourth year of king Nicandros of the Eurypontid line, and arrived at a date for the Return twelve years earlier than that of Eratosthenes. It is seldom possible to know how any chronographer formed his estimate, but Eratosthenes seems to have adapted his figures to a date for the Fall of Troy which he took from what he believed to be an Oriental authority.

An instructive commentary on the value of Greek traditions is Plutarch's statement about the date of the Spartan Lycourgos, who was said to be the son of a king and regent for another, and was certainly the most prominent personage in early Laconian history:

Nothing can be said in general about Lycourgos the legislator that is not disputed, since there are different accounts of his origin, his travels, his end, and particularly of his legislative and constitutional work; and there is least agreement about the time at which the man lived.

Cicero and others adopted the classical expedient for genealogical misfits by assuming that there were two such persons. Some modern criticism goes further and ends in the belief that there was not even one. Yet Lycourgos was not a prehistoric character. Eratosthenes placed him 108 years before the First Olympiad, Callimachos only 56.

The first historians had no notion of an era and little sense of time in its larger aspects. Herodotus, whose purpose was to write the history of the Persian War, does not date the battle of Marathon at all in Greek terms, and some work with paper and pencil is needed to discover from his narrative that the battle of Salamis was fought ten (or eleven?) years after Marathon. Thucydides notes the chronological inaccuracy of Hellanicos in his history of the fifty years between the Persian and Peloponnesian Wars, but what he means is that Hellanicos did not observe the proper sequence of events. He was himself unable to date many important developments in that period, some of which had occurred within his own lifetime. 'About that time' and 'not long after this' are recurring phrases in his summary of quite recent events beyond his own experience. He had occasion to mention the Lelantine War between the Euboian cities of Chalcis and Eretria as the only instance before the Peloponnesian War of a dispute in which the whole of Greece took part on one side or the other, but all that he could say about its date was that it occurred a long while ago. Modern historians place it about 700 B.C.

In his history of the Peloponnesian War Thucydides adopted the old annalistic method, and improved upon it by dividing his years into summers and winters. Annals may be chronologically exact, but their view of history is microscopic. Thucydides did however approach absolute chronology for the first year of the war by the only means available in his time. That year, which we know as 431 B.C., was relatively 'the fifteenth year of the Euboian Truce', and absolutely 'the forty-eighth year of office of the Priestess Chrysis at Argos, the Ephorate of Ainesias at Sparta, and four months from the end of the Archonship of Polydoros at Athens'. The eponymous magistrates of Athens and Sparta are cited because those States were the principals in the war. The mention of the Argive priestess looks like a cautious concession to Hellanicos, who had recently tried to establish the Priestesses of Hera as a national standard of chronology.

Chrysis appears again in Thucydides, but as the central figure in an historical tragedy which is dated by the ninth year of the war, when she must have been about seventy years of age. She fell asleep on duty in the temple of Hera, having left a lighted lamp too near the sacred garlands with which the image of the goddess was adorned. They caught fire, the temple was burnt down, and Chrysis fled to a neighbouring State. Pausanias, writing nearly six hundred years later, says that the Argives did not remove her statue from its place outside the ruined temple, where he saw it.

The inscribed or written lists of the Spartan ephors were said to have begun in the year 755 B.C., those of the Athenian archons in 683. Written records of the Argive temple are not likely to have been older than the eighth century, but the cult of Hera there was of immemorial antiquity, and the succession of priestesses may have gone back to the prehistoric age. No accurate record of the facts could have survived by oral tradition, but fictitious lists were compiled there and elsewhere as soon as the invention of writing provided the necessary instrument. Hellanicos gave them historical expression in his *Priestesses of Hera*. Those venerable ladies held office for life (unless like Chrysis they brought their service to a disastrous end), and Hellanicos used their years for dating real and imaginary events. Few extracts from his book have survived, but two are enough to indicate its range and quality. He is cited by Dionysius of Halicarnassos as placing a migration from Italy to Sicily 'in the third generation before the Trojan War and the twenty-sixth year of the priestess Alcyone', and by the Byzantine pedant John Tzetzes as dating the Fall of Troy by the priestess Callisto.

The first effective move towards a national canon was made by the Sicilian historian Timaios in the third century. He collated the terms of local magistrates with the years of Lacedaimonian kings and Argive priestesses, and with the lists of Olympic victors. Polybius says that his procedure was hypercritical (hence his nickname *Epitimaios*) although he was himself inaccurate. But his alignment of the quadrennial Olympiads with the annual magistracies was a momentous development, for the Olympic Games were the only institution that all Greeks could accept as national.

Olympic festivals are mentioned by Herodotus and Thucydides as historical incidents with no chronological intent. Herodotus says that the battle at Thermopylai was fought at the time of the festival and that was why the Peloponnesians had sent so few troops for the defence of the pass. But he did not identify the Olympiad, which later historians knew as the Seventy-fifth. Thucydides adds the names of Olympic victors to his references. The festival which a Mytilenean delegation attended, in order to make a public protest against Athenian tyranny, was the one at which 'Dorieus of Rhodes was victor for the second time' in some unspecified event. At the Olympiad from which the Spartans were excluded because they had not observed the truce which was proclaimed before each festival, 'Androsthenes of Arcadia won the *pancration* for the first time'. When the Olympiads were numbered, the name of the winner of the short (furlong) foot-race was attached to each as a countersign of identity. Thus the year before the beginning of the Peloponnesian War which Thucydides had to date so clumsily, appears in Diodorus as 'the Archonship of

Pythodoros at Athens and the Eighty-seventh Olympiad, in which Sophron of Ambracia won the *stadion*' (432–1 B.C.).

The Olympiads were numbered and the list of victors was compiled at the end of the fifth century by Hippias of Elis, the pompous professor of all arts who is reduced to absurdity by Socrates in the two Platonic dialogues that bear his name. Plutarch says that his list was based on no convincing evidence, and that statement may well be true; but Hippias did secure the two conditions that are essential to the foundation of an era, precise definition of its initial point and its general acceptance. He established as the First Olympiad that in which Coroibos of Elis won the foot-race, and he completed the series of victors down to his own time, his initial date in terms of the Christian era being 776 B.C. The division of the quadrennial periods into their component years must be credited to Timaios. Plutarch's criticism probably means that this first numbered Olympiad was not in fact the first celebration of the festival; to which Hippias would doubtless have replied that it was the first to which the name of a victor could be plausibly attached. The fact that Coroibos and some at least of his early successors could be named must mean that some material evidence of them was available. If the beginning of the list had been wholly fictitious, Hippias could have taken it back to a much earlier date.

Myth attributed the foundation of the Games to the gods, or to Endymion, the Man in the Moon. Legend assigned it to Pelops or Heracles, tradition to a shadowy king of Elis, Iphitos, in association with that equally vague personage, Lycourgos of Sparta. The Olympiad of Iphitos (which was never included in the chronological notation) was placed by Eratosthenes 108 years before the Olympiad of Coroibos.

The story of the establishment or restoration of the festival by Iphitos and Lycourgos seems to have been invented to support the claims of Elis to control the festival and of Sparta to control Elis. To support the story the Eleians showed an inscription on a bronze discus. That document, which Aristotle was said to have accepted as authentic, was seen by Pausanias in the temple of Hera at Olympia. The text was inscribed spirally on the disk and contained the terms of the Panhellenic truce which was proclaimed before each festival. It was certainly a forgery, for no such elaborate and precise inscription could have existed in the ninth century. Nor was it the only forgery of its kind.

In his account of the Phoenician origins of the Greek alphabet Herodotus says that he had seen 'Cadmeian letters' engraved on tripods in the temple of Ismenian Apollo at Thebes, and quotes three of the inscriptions, which were in hexameter verse. One stated that the tripod was dedicated by Amphitryon on his return from his Teleboian expedition, that is to say, before the birth of his son Heracles:

Amphitryon set me here from the spoils of the Teleboians.

Another recorded a dedication by one Scaios, a pugilist, identified by Herodotus as a contemporary of Oidipous, and the third was from Laodamas, who was king of Thebes at the time of the second Argive attack as related in the *Epigonoi.* The Hecataian dates of these events, as quoted by Herodotus elsewhere, would be about 1360 and 1260 B.C.

Even if the prehistoric statements, which agree with the legends, had been matters of fact, it is certain that the epic hexameter had not been developed at that time and that the Greek alphabet had not been invented. It is of course possible that bronze tripods might have been found bearing long dedications in Mycenean or Cypriote script and in the Greek language, but hardly three of the same kind in one place. It is also certain that the historical Greeks could not read nor even recognise the prehistoric scripts (Plate 2). If the inscriptions were unintelligible, their professed interpretation by the priests was false; but Herodotus implies that he read the texts and says that the characters were 'for the most part like the Ionian', which he could not have done if they had been Mycenean or Cypriote. Pausanias saw a tripod in the same temple purporting to have been dedicated by Heracles when he had served there as a boy priest. It may have been an addition to the series or a new interpretation of a text that Herodotus saw. The best that can be said for the Theban tripods is that they may have been prehistoric antiquities to which archaic Greek inscriptions had been added.

The repute of these interesting documents extended to their custodians and interpreters, the priests of Apollo at Thebes, who became recognised authorities in epigraphical and linguistic scholarship. The author of the Aristotelian *Book of Wonders* tells the story of an inscribed stone that was found in the country of the Ainianes, near Hypata in the northern Achaia:

As it bore writing in ancient characters and the Ainianes wanted to know to whom it belonged, they deputed certain persons to take it to Athens. But as they passed through Boiotia and communicated the purpose of their mission to some of their hosts there, the deputies were conducted to the Ismeneion at Thebes, where the Boiotians said the meaning of the writing could most easily be found, adding that there were in that temple some ancient dedications with letters similar in form to those of the stone in question. Whence the Ainianes say that having found an explanation of the object of their enquiry, they wrote down the following verses from what was previously known to them:

> Heracles founded the shrine for Cythera Phersephaässê,
> Driving the herds of Geryon, the spoils from Erytheia,

and so on for four more lines.

The Theban priests seem to have made a speciality of identifying Heracleid relics: a wise choice, since he was born at Thebes and was also a national hero. The Spartans in the fifth century showed a gold cup which Zeus had given to Alcmena, the mother of Heracles, on the occasion of his nocturnal visit. That must have come from Thebes, and was doubtless authenticated by an appropriate inscription.

One of the speakers in Plutarch's Dialogue *On the Genius of Socrates* is represented as having been present at the discovery, in the fourth century, of the grave of Alcmena at Haliartos in Boiotia, which was evidently identified by an inscription found in it,

and of which the contents were appropriated by the Spartan king
Agesilaos, as his ancestral property:

The tomb contained beside the body a small bronze armlet and
two jars of pottery filled with earth which age had made as com-
pact and hard as stone. There was a bronze tablet inscribed with
many letters marvellously old, for nothing could be made of them
although they showed up clearly when the bronze was washed.
The style of the writing was strange and foreign, most like the
Egyptian. So Agesilaos, as they say, sent copies of it to the king
(of Egypt), asking him to show them to the priests, in case they
could understand them. The people of Haliartos think that the
great famine and the overflow of their lake did not occur naturally, but were retribution provoked by them in allowing the tomb
to be opened. The Lacedaimonians too did not escape retribution,
for they sent a person to fill in the grave and make libations to
Alcmena and Aleos in accordance with some oracle, though they
did not know who Aleos might be.

This is certainly a reference to the Mycenean script. Another is
the circumstantial story of the discovery at Cnossos of the original
Journal of the Trojan War of Dictys of Crete. The script, written
there on clay tablets, was recognised by the Emperor Nero as
Phoenician, and duly translated into Greek by Phoenician scholars. Another pre-Homeric impostor, Corinnos of Troy, wrote his
contemporary history of the war in 'the Dorian script which
Palamedes had invented'. That was probably a mere name, like
Palamedes himself, and had no particular significance.

There was indeed no room for any native script, Minoan, Mycenean or Dorian, in Greek reconstructions of history. The historical Greeks knew that their alphabet was Phoenician, as the
names of its letters must have told them; but they did not know
how or when they had come by it, and assumed its use in remote
prehistoric times. Since Cadmos of Thebes was a mythical Phoenician immigrant, its introduction was generally attributed to him,
and he was placed by the mythographical historians seven or eight
generations before the Trojan War, in modern terms about

1500 B.C. The people of Greece were then using the Minoan syllabic script, if they used any, and the Western Semitic languages
were being written in cuneiform. The Phoenician alphabet was
devised between that time and the eleventh century, when it begins to appear in Syrian inscriptions. Greek knowledge and memory of the Minoan and Mycenean scripts were completely lost in
the cultural relapse that followed the Dorian invasion, although a
derivative syllabic script was current in Cyprus until the fifth
century (Plate 2).

Relics of legendary heroes and heroines were shown in many
temples and were regarded with respect or amusement according
to the piety or common sense of the observer. Among the more
fantastic were the swan's egg laid by Leda, which was hung with
ribbons from the ceiling of a temple at Sparta, and the tusks of the
Calydonian boar, which Augustus removed from Tegea in Arcadia to Rome, where one of them, 'exactly half a fathom long'
according to Pausanias, was preserved in the Imperial gardens.
The hide was left in the temple, where Pausanias saw it 'very much
decayed by age and quite bare of bristles'. A letter sent home from
Troy by Sarpedon and kept in some temple in Lycia puzzled Pliny
for a wrong reason, because it was written on papyrus. Many of
these objects must have been genuine antiquities, and could offer
archaeological information even to Pausanias, who says on one
occasion:

That all weapons in the Heroic Age were bronze is shown by
Homer, and I am confirmed in this belief by the spear of Achilles,
which is dedicated in the temple of Athena at Phaselis, and the
sword of Memnon in the temple of Asclepios at Nicomedia, for
the blade and the spike on the butt of the spear and the whole of
the sword are of bronze.

Historical fraud began when such objects were inscribed by their
possessors with statements purporting to be contemporary with
them, or when inscriptions in unintelligible scripts or languages
were translated into Greek. One or both of these processes must
have been applied to the Theban tripods.

3

PUBLIC INSTRUCTION

The Chronicle of Lindos – epigraphic forgeries – the priests of Halicarnassos – Dorian genealogical fictions – religious credulity – public inscriptions – the Parian Marble – prehistoric Athenian kings – historical tradition – Pheidon of Argos – day of the Fall of Troy.

A whole catalogue of antiquarian forgeries belonging to the temple of Athena was found in 1904 by a Danish expedition at Lindos in Rhodes. This is a long inscription on marble, which is known as the Lindian Chronicle. It was placed in the temple by the City Council in the year 99 B.C., and records treasures dedicated to Athena by prehistoric and historical persons. The prehistoric documents were authenticated by fraudulent inscriptions.

The prescript recites the decree authorising the preparation of the list, and directs that since most of the ancient offerings had perished in course of time (the temple was burnt out at the beginning of the fourth century), their descriptions should be repeated on the stone from extant archives and publications. The compiler records the inscriptions which had been engraved on the objects by their dedicators, and refers to the publication of each piece in earlier literature. The list of prehistoric treasures with their dedicatory inscriptions is translated here, but the compiler's references to previous publications is repeated only in the fifth entry (Heracles), where all the authorities are represented. The name of the dedicator comes first in each entry.

THESE PERSONS MADE DEDICATIONS TO ATHENA

LINDOS, a cup of which nobody could know the material, inscribed: *Lindos to Athena Polias and Zeus Polieus.* [Lindos was the pre-Dorian eponym of the city, a mythological personage. The material of the cup had not been noted in the earlier records.]

The TELCHEINES, a vessel of which nobody could know the material, inscribed: *The Telcheines to Athena Polias and Zeus Polieus, a tithe of their handiwork.* [The Telcheines were mythical craftsmen of Rhodes, like the Dactyls of Crete and Phrygia.]

CADMOS, a bronze cauldron inscribed with Phoenician letters.

MINOS, a silver goblet, inscribed: *Minos to Athena Polias and Zeus Polieus.*

HERACLES, two shields, one covered with leather, the other with bronze. On the leathern shield, *Heracles, the shield of Eurypylos, from the Meropes*; on the bronze-plated one, *Heracles, the shield of Laomedon, from the Teucrians, to Athena Polias and Zeus Polieus*; as described by Xenagoras in the first book of his *Chronicle*, by Gorgon in the first book of his *Rhodes*, by Nicasylos in the third book of his *Chronicle*, by Hegesias in his *Encomion of Rhodes*, by Aielouros in his book *On the War against the Exagiades*, by Phaennos in his *Lindos*, by Gorgosthenes in his *Report*, by Hieroboulos in his *Report*. [The shield of Laomedon was a trophy of the first Trojan War, in which Heracles and Telamon sacked the city. Eurypylos was king in the island of Cos, to which Heracles had been driven by storm on his way back from Troy.]

TLEPOLEMOS, a cup, a votive offering, inscribed: *Tlepolemos to Athena Polias and Zeus Polieus, a votive offering.* [Tlepolemos, son of Heracles, is king of Rhodes in the Homeric *Catalogue of Ships*. The vow was evidently related to his safe return, but he was killed by Sarpedon in the fifth book of the *Iliad*.]

RHESOS, a gold goblet, inscribed: *Rhesos, a deposit, to be redeemed by whoever* ... [Rhesos was the Thracian prince who was killed by Odysseus and Diomedes in their night raid as related in the tenth book of the *Iliad*.]

TELEPHOS, a cup with gold centre-piece, inscribed: *Telephos to Athena, a propitiatory offering as the Lycian Apollo enjoined.* [Telephos, king of Teuthrania in Asia, was the son of Heracles and Augê. The propitiation was probably in respect of his being a child of sin, his mother having been priestess of Athena at Tegea in Arcadia. The oracle of the Lycian Apollo was at Patara.]

Those who made the expedition to Ilion with Tlepolemos, nine shields, nine daggers, nine helmets, nine pairs of greaves, the shields inscribed: *Those who made the expedition to Ilion with Tlepolemos, to Athena of Lindos, choice spoils from Troy.* [Tlepolemos leads nine ships to Troy in the Homeric *Catalogue*.]

MENELAOS, a helmet, inscribed: *Menelaos, the helmet of Alexander.* [This was the helmet which Menelaos pulled off the head of Paris and threw to the Greeks in their duel in the third book of the *Iliad*.]

HELEN, a pair of bracelets, inscribed: *Helen to Athena.*

CANOPOS, the helmsman of Menelaos, his steering-oars, inscribed: *Canopos to Athena Polias.*

MERIONES, a silver quiver, inscribed: *Meriones son of Molos, choice spoil from Troy.*

TEUCROS, a quiver inscribed: *Teucros, the quiver of Pandaros.* Theotimos says that he also dedicated the bow. [The bow and arrows of Pandaros were shown in the temple of Apollo at Sicyon, and doubtless in other places.]

The inscription is in the Doric dialect of Rhodes, but the Dorian origins of the Rhodian cities are ignored in these prehistoric fictions. The catalogue was the work of Timacidas of Rhodes, an antiquary and literary critic who is often quoted by Athenaeus and the scholiasts. Most of the earlier authorities whom he cites were local historians.

Local chronicles (*Hôroi*) were the first productions of Ionian prose writing. They took their form and the material for their own times from civic lists of magistrates and events associated with their names. Those records did not go as far back as the foundation of the cities, and the gap above them was filled from more or less vague traditions. The Asiatic colonies began where the Heroic Age ended. Beyond that point the poetical statements of the epics were accepted as historical, and were supported by the material evidence of the temple forgeries, which were themselves constructed from the epic narratives.

Equally fraudulent in intent and in effect were monumental inscriptions in temples and elsewhere, of which the content was fictitious but which may not have been forgeries in the sense that they purported to be contemporary with the persons whom they celebrated. The Lacedaimonian king-lists were traditional documents, and all the imaginative elements which they contained need not have been devised at any one moment. But the records of the prehistoric Argive priestesses were deliberate inventions. They may have been the work of many heads and hands, but they received their final polish from the disciplined ingenuity of Hellanicos.

An extant temple-record of this kind comes from Halicarnassos in Caria. It is a list of twenty-seven priests of Poseidon with their years of office in hereditary succession from Telamon, son of Poseidon, and is a copy, made apparently in the first century A.D., of an earlier inscription which must have been old enough to need replacement. The first part of the text is translated here:

Ordered that there be copied from the ancient stone which stands beside the statues of Poseidon Isthmios the list of those who have been from the foundation of the city hereditary priests in the temple of Poseidon which was dedicated to Poseidon and Apollo by those who led the colony from Troizen.

THE PRIESTS OF POSEIDON ON THE STONE
ARE THESE

TELAMON SON OF POSEIDON	12 years
ANTIDIOS SON OF TELAMON	27
HYPERES SON OF TELAMON	9
ALCYONEUS SON OF TELAMON	12
TELAMON SON OF ANTIDIOS	22
HYRIEUS SON OF ANTIDIOS	8
ANTHEUS SON OF ALCYONEUS	19

and so on for twenty more holders of the office. The form of inheritance is remarkable, and doubtless records the historical fact that brother succeeded brother in each generation. The prescript indicates that this was the beginning of a list of which the end was contemporary with the decree, and which must have covered a

period of at least thirteen hundred years. If all the tenures of office
were on this scale, it would have contained about ninety names.

Pausanias says that the Troizenians were second to none in
making much of their local history. He gathered from them that
two of their first kings, Hyperes and Anthes, were sons of Poseidon
and a daughter of Atlas, Alcyonê. Strabo says that on the arrival of
Troizen, the eponym, and Pittheus, sons of Pelops, Anthes left his
kingdom and founded Halicarnassos. Pelops in the legends was
grandfather or great-grandfather of Agamemnon, and should
have lived about a century before the Trojan War. The date of
these events would therefore be, in the old chronology quoted by
Herodotus, about 1300 B.C. But Strabo also says, in another place
that Halicarnassos, being a Dorian colony, did not exist at the time
of the Trojan War.

Herodotus, who was a native of Halicarnassos and records some
of its peculiarities at length, says of its origin: 'Halicarnassos was a
Dorian colony from Troizen.' The fiction of a prehistoric Greek
foundation could not have been accepted when Herodotus wrote
or he would surely have noted it, considering that he has so much
to say about a pre-Dorian settlement in Thera and that Halicarnassos was his own birthplace. The story probably began with
a fifth-century enlargement of Troizenian history in the manner
of Hellanicos, and the colony set up this monumental evidence to
support it. The cities in Rhodes were also founded by Dorian
colonists, and retained their original dialect, as Halicarnassos did
not. But Lindos, as we have seen, claimed a mythical eponym, and
represented its famous temple of Athena as existing long before
the Trojan War.

Dorian places, like Dorian persons, sought pre-Dorian origins
when the epic poets had made the nation conscious of its heroic
ancestry. Herodotus tells a tale of the Spartan king Cleomenes who
had come to Athens on a military mission and attempted to enter
the temple of Athena on the Acropolis. The priestess, rising from
her throne, told him that Dorian strangers were not permitted to
set foot on that holy ground. To which the king replied: 'Madam,

3   Part of the rock-sculpture of Behistun. Under the sign of Ahura-
mazda nine kings, arms tied behind their backs, face Dareios, whose
foot is on the neck of the rebel Gaumata.

4 Rock-cut relief in the gorge of Kara Bel, near Smyrna. This monument, mentioned by Herodotus, proves that Hittite influence extended as far as the Aegean coast. From a drawing made in 1834.

I am not a Dorian, I am an Achaian', meaning, of course, that he was a returned Heracleid.

Halicarnassos therefore aspired, like Lindos, to a longer lineage than the Spartan kings, and expressed it in the pre-Pelopid names of the temple-list. Since the first priest Telamon is a son of Poseidon, he is represented as a brother of the founder, Anthes. His son Hyperes gets his name from his Troizenian uncle, Alcyoneus commemorates his mythical grandmother, and Anthes is revived in the next generation.

These Halicarnassian and Rhodian inscriptions were civic documents and also had religious sanction. The producers of the Lindian and Theban dedications had epic authority for the names, but they knew that their inscriptions were false, as did the inventors of the prehistoric Halicarnassian priests and years of office. There was a wide gulf between the mentality of the literary artists who produced these fictions, and that of the general public and even of historians who received them as facts. Herodotus accepted the Theban documents as authentic records of Heracles, and was cautious in his criticisms of religious fable. He ends a rational discussion of a superhuman feat of Heracles with a kind of prayer: 'In saying so much about these matters, may I incur no displeasure of god or hero.' Pausanias was a man of lesser intelligence, but he lived in a much later and more sophisticated age, was exceptionally well educated and widely travelled. Yet his piety made him accept historical and religious phenomena which were manifestly ridiculous.

An extreme instance is his statement about the pet deer of Artemis at Lycosoura in Arcadia, which was last seen by one Arcesilaos, a descendant in the ninth generation of Leocydes who commanded the Arcadians with Aratos in the middle of the third century B.C. That would make the date of Arcesilaos about the end of the first century. Pausanias says that at this time the deer was old and feeble: 'On its neck was a collar, and on the collar an inscription' (as always, in hexameter verse):

> *I was caught as a fawn when Agapenor was at Ilion.*

His comment is: 'This story proves that the deer is a much longer-lived animal even than the elephant.' By the chronology of Eratosthenes this specimen would have been about twelve hundred years old.

Monumental inscriptions were a form of publicity which was necessarily used in the ancient world for lists of magistrates, legal enactments, treaties, and other official documents of which general knowledge was desirable. It was also used for private announcements which their authors designed for public instruction or to perpetuate their own achievements. The cutting of these long texts in stone may seem to have been a formidable and costly operation, but marble and masons were cheap, and one inscription in the author's locality would be more effective than a large number of manuscripts.

The practice of publishing astronomical and chronological theories in this form was so familiar that the word for placard (*parapêgma*) could be used for any such formal scheme. Thus Diodorus, lamenting the difficulties of writing prehistoric history, says that he could not find any reliable *parapêgma* of dates before the Trojan War: not that they were rare, but they did not agree with one another. The systems so published seem generally to have been formulated by individual authors who prefixed their names to the texts. Plutarch cites the authority of an inscription preserved at Sicyon which dated mythical achievements in music and poetry by the years of Argive priestesses. It was probably excerpted from the famous chronological treatise of Hellanicos.

These personal advertisements were not well received by professional historians. Polybius makes contemptuous reference to 'people who note casual occurrences in chronographies posted up on walls for public instruction'. An ambitious *parapêgma* of this kind has survived in a long inscription which is usually known, from the island in which it was found and the stone in which it is cut, as the Parian Marble.

This chronicle is a dated record of some notable events in imaginary and real Greek history from the reign of Cecrops, the first mythical king of Athens, to the archonship of Diognetos in the year which corresponds to 264/3 B.C. The larger part of the inscription must have been among the first Greek antiquities brought to this country as such. It was bought in Smyrna for the Earl of Arundel by William Petty, physician of the English Embassy to the Ottoman Porte in the time of King Charles I. It arrived in London in 1627 and was placed in Arundel House in the Strand. In the following year it was published by the distinguished scholar and jurist John Selden, to whose competence and diligence we owe our knowledge of the prehistoric portion of the text.

Arundel House was abandoned by the Howard family during the Civil War, and the Greek marbles suffered from the attentions of its Parliamentary occupants. The Chronicle was cut in two, its upper half was used to repair a fireplace and has not been heard of since then. The remaining Arundel Marbles, with the lower half of the Chronicle, were given to the University of Oxford by Henry Howard, grandson of the Earl, in 1667, and are now in the Ashmolean Museum. A third piece of the inscription, found in Paros in 1897, brings the entries down to the year 299/8 B.C.

The stone is 32 inches wide and when complete was about 7 feet high. The text of the portion that was destroyed in London is preserved in Selden's copy, so far as the scholarship and epigraphic experience of his day could reproduce it. Selden explains that many letters had completely disappeared, others were only partially visible. Subsequent editors have worked to good effect on his copy, and the text as now established contains the essential elements of most of the prehistoric entries.

The literary content of the Chronicle was compiled from current authorities, general histories, annals of Attica (*Atthids*), handbooks of literature and catalogues of discoveries and inventions. The chronological scheme seems to have been the compiler's contribution and the innovation which he wished to bring to public notice. He devised a true era, though a merely personal one, its terminal point being the archonship of Diognetos at Athens in the year corresponding to 264/3 B.C. All his events are fixed by counting upwards from that date, as years B.C. are counted in the Christian era. He also used the current chronological canon of the annual Athenian archons, and for the times before their records began, the reigns of the Athenian kings. Since the Parian Chronicle is not an easily accessible document and exists only in its original Greek, a translation of all the prehistoric entries may be acceptable here.

The words in brackets are those that can be safely restored from the context or from odd letters that can be read. The dotted lines represent gaps in the text of which the original content cannot be so restored.

EPOCH	TEXT	DATE B.C.
I	... [name of compiler lost] ... inscribed this record of (former times) from Cecrops the first king of Athens to the archonships of ... in Paros and Diognetos at Athens.	264/3
1	Since Cecrops was king at Athens and the country previously called Acticê after Actaios the authochthon received the name of Cecropia, 1318 years =	1582
2	Since Deucalion was king in Leucoreia by Parnassos, in the reign of Cecrops at Athens, 1310 years =	1574
3	Since Ares and Poseidon came to judgment at Athens on account of Halirrhothios son of Poseidon, and the place of judgment received the name of Areiopagos, in the reign of Cranaos at Athens, 1268 years =	1532
4	Since the flood occurred in the time of Deucalion, and Deucalion fled from the waters from Leu-	

coreia to Athens ... and founded the temple of
Olympian Zeus and offered the sacrifice for
safety, in the reign of Cranaos at Athens,

1265 years = 1529

5   Since Amphictyon son of Deucalion was king at
Thermopylai and brought together the people
who dwelt around the sanctuary, and gave their
names to the Amphictyons and to Pylaia where
the Amphictyons still sacrifice, in the reign of
Amphictyon at Athens,   1258 years = 1522

6   Since Hellen son of Deucalion was king of
Phthiotis and the people previously called Greeks
were named Hellenes and the Games ... , in the
reign of Amphictyon at Athens,   1257 years = 1521

7   Since Cadmos son of Agenor came to Thebes ...
and built the Cadmeia, in the reign of Amphictyon at Athens,   1255 years = 1519

8   Since (Cilix and Phoinix sons of Agenor) were
kings in (Cilicia and) Phoenicia, in the reign of
Amphictyon at Athens,   1252 years = 1516

9   Since a ship ... sailed from Egypt to Greece and
was called a pentecontor, and the daughters of
Danaos ... and Helicê and Archedicê were selected from the rest by lot ... and offered sacrifice
on the shore at Lindos in Rhodes during the
voyage, in the reign of (Erichthonios at Athens),

1247 years = 1511

10 Since Erichthonios harnessed a chariot at the first
celebration of the Panathenaic Festival, and
instituted the Games, and gave the Athenians
their name, and ... of the Mother (of the gods)
was revealed in Cybela, and the Phrygian Hyagnis
invented flutes ... and first played the mode that
is called Phrygian and other music of the
Mother, Dionysos, Pan, and the ... , in the reign

of Erichthonios who harnessed the chariot at
Athens,   1242 years = 1506

11   Since (the first) Minos (was king in Crete and)
founded ... , and iron-working was invented in
Ida, the inventors being the Idaian Dactyls Cel-
mios and ... , in the reign of Pandion at Athens,
                             (years) = 1462–
                                                  1423

12   Since Demeter came to Athens and (instituted)
harvest, and (the first Proerosia was performed
by instruction of) Triptolemos son of Celeos and
Neaira, in the reign of Erichtheus at Athens,
                             1146 years = 1410

13   Since Triptolemos ... sowed in the place called
Rharia at Eleusis, in the reign of Erichtheus at
Athens,   1145 years = 1409

14   (Since ...) produced his own poetry, the Rape of
Corê and Demeter's Quest, and the ... of those
who received the harvest, in the reign of Erichtheus at Athens,   1135 years = 1399

15   (Since ...) produced the Mysteries at Eleusis and
published the poems of ... Mousaios, in the reign
of Erichtheus son of Pandion at Athens,
                                 (years) = 1398–
                                                 1373

16   Since purification was first instituted ... , in the
reign of Pandion son of Cecrops at Athens,
                             1062 years = 1326

17   Since the gymnastic (contest) at Eleusis, ... the
Lycaia in Arcadia was established and ... of
Lycaon were given ... to the Hellenes, in the
reign of Pandion son of Cecrops at Athens,
                                 (years) = 1325–
                                                 1308

18 Since ... Heracles ... , in the reign of Aigeus at
Athens,   (years) = 1307–
1296

19 Since harvests (failed) at Athens and Apollo
directed the Athenians who consulted the oracle
to make (amends) ... which Minos should demand, in the reign of Aigeus at Athens,
1031 years = 1295

20 Since Theseus ... became king at Athens and
brought the twelve townships together and gave
them (one) constitution and the democracy, and
... founded the Isthmian Games after killing
Sinis,   995 years = 1259

21 Since the Amazons (invaded Attica), in the reign
of Theseus at Athens,   992 years = 1256

22 Since the Argives with Adrastos (attacked
Thebes) and founded the Games at (Nemea) ... ,
in the reign of Theseus at Athens, 987 years = 1251

23 Since the Hellenes made the expedition to Troy
in the thirteenth year of the reign of Menestheus
at Athens,   954 years = 1218

24 Since Troy fell in the (twenty–)second year of
the reign of Menestheus at Athens, on the seventh
day from the end of the month Thargelion,
945 years = 1209

25 Since Orestes ... (and Erigonê) daughter of Aigisthos (came to judgment) at the Areiopagos (on
account of Aigisthos and Clytaimnestra) and
Orestes won the suit ... in the reign of Demophon at Athens,   9(44) years = 1208

26 Since Teucros founded (Salamis) in Cyprus, in
the reign of Demophon at Athens,   938 years = 1202

27 Since Neleus founded (Miletos and all the rest of

Ionia), Ephesos, Erythrai, Clazomenai ... Colophon, Myous ... Samos ... , and the Panionia was
established, in the reign of (Medon) at Athens,
                              (82)3 years = 1087

28   Since the poet Hesiod (lived), in the reign of ...
     at Athens,   67(3) years = 937

29   Since the poet Homer lived, in the reign of Diog-
     netos at Athens,   643 years = 907

30   Since Pheidon of Argos established (weights and
     measures) and coined silver in Aigina, being
     eleventh in descent from Heracles, in the reign of
     Pherecles at Athens,   631 years = 895

The list of Athenian kings used by the chronicler as his sub-
sidiary canon was the same as that quoted by Eusebius from
Castor:

CASTOR ON THE KINGDOM OF THE ATHENIANS

		(Years B.C. from dates in Chronicle)
Cecrops I	50 years	1582
Cranaos	9	1532
Amphictyon	10	1522
Erichthonios	50	1511
Pandion I	40	(1462)
Erichtheus	50	1410
Cecrops II	40	(1373)
Pandion II	25	1326
Aigeus	48	1295
Theseus	29	1259
Menestheus	22	1231
Demophon	33	1208

These kings are not comparable historically with those of the
Lacedaimonian dynasties. Theirs was a traditional list beginning
with fictitious elements but ending with contemporary facts; the

Athenian kings were prehistoric and mainly or wholly mythical. Demophon and Menestheus were mere names connecting Athens with the Trojan legend and perhaps invented for that purpose. The sons of Theseus are not mentioned by Homer, but in the *Iphigeneia in Aulis* of Euripides, Demophon has taken the place of Menestheus as leader of the Athenian contingent.

Theseus became a brilliant figure of Attic folk-lore and literature, but is little more in himself than a provincial Heracles. His name (the 'Founder') is suspiciously like his reputed political achievements (*Epoch* 20), which are not easily reconciled with his amatory and predatory adventures. His father Aigeus, eponym of the Aegean Sea, has a name which was a cult-title of Poseidon; his mother, Aithra, and his first recorded love, Ariadne, have names of goddesses. All the predecessors of Aigeus except Amphictyon seem to have been local gods. Erichthonios and Erichtheus are two forms of the name of an earth-god, who was identified with Poseidon in the old sanctuary of the Erechtheion. Cecrops was worshipped in Boiotia as well as in Attica: he was associated with Athena and represented as a semi-serpentine monster.

Amphictyon is also mythical, but he was a stranger at Athens, introduced for political reasons and never properly assimilated. He was the eponymous hero of the Amphictyonic Council which had its sanctuary at Anthela near Thermopylai and was concerned with religious administration at Delphi. The Amphictyons were thought to have been so named because they 'dwelt around' the sanctuary. The connection of Amphictyon with Deucalion at Thermopylai (*Epoch* 6) was an obvious piece of local genealogy; the unlikely connection of father and son with Attica (*Epoch* 4) was meant to claim prominent places for Athens in Delphic management and Hellenic origins. The chronicler made two persons of Amphictyon king at Thermopylai and Amphictyon king at Athens, but their actual separation was impossible, particularly so when Deucalion himself had been transported to Athens by his flood.

The story of Deucalion's flood probably had its origin in a local catastrophe in Boiotia, where inundation was frequent and the formation of the huge Copaic Lake had followed the destruction of a Minoan drainage system. Deucalion's original landing-place was Mount Parnassos. His flood became in course of time a national and even an international event, and he and his wife Pyrrha came to safety at many other places in Greece: Athens, Argos, Othrys, Dodona and elsewhere. The Athenians showed Pausanias Deucalion's grave and the hole in a rock down which the flood-waters had run away. As the father of Hellen (*Epoch* 6), Deucalion was the ancestor of all true Greeks. But he was not properly at home at Athens.

The conventional claim of Attic historians, which Thucydides makes even for prehistoric times, that 'Athens was always inhabited by the same people: fugitives from other parts of Greece came there for security and added to the greatness of the city', is hardly borne out by this ragged list of kings, which was in no sense a dynasty. If ancient tradition could have survived anywhere, it should have been in Attica, but these names show that the Athenians had no prehistoric memories at all.

The doubling of Cecrops and Pandion (*Epoch* 16) was a late development, unknown to Herodotus and Thucydides. It was an awkward way out of difficulties created by progressive genealogical theories and static chronology. In the old list there were 10 kings from Cecrops to Demophon, and their sum of years was 406: that is to say, the chronology was based on the generation of 40 years. When the 33-year generation was generally recognised, the Athenians adapted it by duplicating two of their kings, since the sum of years could not be altered and new names could not be added. The doubling of Minos (*Epochs* 11 *and* 19), which was also unknown to Herodotus and Thucydides, became necessary when the new ethnographical genealogies diverged from the old heroic pedigrees. Minos was the grandfather of Idomeneus, who fought at Troy, but he was also a son of the Phoenician Europa, who was a sister of Cadmos (*Epochs* 7 *and* 8), and these two identities were three generations apart. The same tension operating on Sarpedon, the brother of Minos, was released by a miracle of Zeus (page 93).

The last three events recorded on this lost portion of the stone were not mythical or legendary but traditional. The dates assigned to Homer and Hesiod (*Epochs* 28 *and* 29) are not very far from those of Herodotus, and represent a moderate conjecture. It is interesting to note that Hesiod is placed one generation before Homer. Most ancient opinion made them contemporary; some gave them a genealogy which made them cousins; but modern criticism puts Homer definitely before Hesiod. They could have had little personal impact on the generations in which they lived. Their works were published gradually and anonymously (the use of Hesiod's name in the current proem to the *Theogony* is at least ambiguous), and were followed by and confused with many poems by other authors in the same style. But Pheidon of Argos (*Epoch* 30) was a very different person, and his date, if any, ought to have been kept in memory and would have been recorded in writing, if any such records had been made.

Pheidon was remembered as the great king who held the Argive hegemony of the Peloponnese against the rising power of Sparta. If there had been no uncertainty about his date, and no manipulation of written records, we could accept the Eleian entry in the Olympic register, as reported by Pausanias, to the effect that the Eighth Olympiad (= 748 B.C.) was null and void (an *anolympiad*) because Pheidon had supported the Pisatans in seizing control of the sanctuary. The Parian chronicler supports his much earlier date (= 895 B.C.) by the statement that Pheidon was eleventh in descent from Heracles.

The Dorian royal house of Argos traced its Heracleid line through Temenos, one of the three brothers who were said to have led the Dorian invasion, the others being Aristodemos, father of the Spartan twins, and Cresphontes who took Messenia as his allotted portion. Pheidon would thus be seventh from Temenos. Strabo says that Ephoros placed him in the tenth generation from Temenos. Herodotus makes a son of Pheidon one of the suitors for the hand of Agaristê, daughter of Cleisthenes of Sicyon. It is true that the Wooing of Agaristê was one of the Panhellenic occasions (perhaps the last), like the Voyage of the Argo, the Hunting of the Calydonian Boar, or the Siege of Troy, at which the participants were not necessarily contemporary with one another, but Herodotus is very definite about Pheidon in this passage. He says that Leocedes 'was the son of that Pheidon who established weights and measures throughout the Peloponnese and was the most arrogant of all the Greeks: he who displaced the Eleian controllers of the Olympic festival and directed the games himself'. The successful suitor of Agaristê, and perhaps the only real one, was Megacles of Athens, great-grandfather of Pericles. Herodotus therefore dated Pheidon four or five generations before his own time, about 600 B.C. We have thus three ancient dates for Pheidon, apart from those that might be calculated from the genealogies, covering a period of three hundred years: 895 (the Parian chronicler), 748 (the Olympic register), and 600 B.C. (Herodotus). If Greek folk-memory could be so grossly at fault within three or four hundred years of the lifetime of an outstanding historical personage, it is manifestly futile to look for chronological reality in computations based on prehistoric legend.

The definition of the month and day of the Fall of Troy (*Epoch* 24) offers an amusing insight into ancient scientific method. The process began with a line in the *Little Iliad*: 'It was the middle of the night and a bright moon was shining'. That guileless statement was twisted by an exchange of prepositions, *ana* (up) for *epi* (on), to mean that a bright moon was rising; and a slight extension of the sense made the bright moon a full moon. The full moon cannot of course rise at midnight, but the time when it comes nearest to doing so, that is to say when a midnight rising comes nearest to the full moon, is said to be in the last lunation before the summer solstice. The Greeks were unable to compute the astronomical conditions of this phenomenon, but they identified it empirically as to the day, with a possible variation of one month. The scholiast on the *Hecuba* of Euripides explains that such a moon rises at midnight on the eighth day from the end of the month and not on any other day, and that Euripides recognised that fact. Euripides merely makes his Chorus of Trojan Women say, 'In the middle of the night I was destroyed.' A further statement of the scholiast implies that another day, the twelfth of Thargelion, adopted by Hellanicos and others, was not derived from lunar observation.

The astronomical date is defined at length by Dionysius:

Troy was taken towards the close of summer, 17 days before the solstice, on the eighth day from the end of the month Thargelion by the Attic calendar. There remained 20 days after the solstice to complete that year.

The Attic year began at midsummer. The day specified in the Parian Chronicle, the seventh from the end of Thargelion (May – June), is the same as this, the apparent discrepancy being due to the allocation of the same night to different days. The Greek day began at sunset, the Roman day at midnight. The date expressed in modern terms is June 5th, 1209 B.C.

This exercise in false precision attracted much attention from Early Christian and Byzantine writers. It is mentioned by Clement of Alexandria, who quotes the statement that the moon was full, by Eusebius in his *Preparation of the Gospel*, and by John Tzetzes in his doggerel poem *Posthomerica*. Tzetzes follows Hellanicos for the day, the twelfth of Thargelion, and adds the name of the Argive priestess at the time, Callisto (he wrote 'Athens' by mistake). Those who agreed with the Parian chronicler in the day, but placed it in the following month of Scirophorion, made it the Fourth of July.

4

HISTORY AND ROMANCE

Year of the Fall of Troy – the Locrian Maidens – human sacrifice – ritual stone-throwing – methods of chronological computation – Ctesias – Oriental history – kings of the Medes – kings of the Assyrians – chronology of Ctesias – Ninos, Semiramis and Sesostris – royal Persian records – cuneiform texts – the monument of Behistun – Memnon at Troy – chronology of Eratosthenes – archaeological evidence – Egyptian and Hittite records – Achaians.

There was more room for disagreement about the year of the Fall of Troy. Some of the dates adopted by various authorities (if that name may be given to them in this context) are recorded by later writers, and a few are extant in their own works. The estimates and their sources are:

	Years B.C.
Douris of Samos, fourth century (Clement of Alexandria)	1334
'Herodotean' *Life of Homer*	1270
Herodotus, fifth century	about 1250
Dicaiarchos, fourth century (Scholiast on Apollonius Rhodius)	1212
Parian Chronicle, third century	1209
Thrasyllos (Clement)	1194
Timaios, third century (Censorinus)	1193
Ctesias, fifth century (Diodorus, Agathias)	about 1183
Eratosthenes, third century (Diodorus, Clement)	1183
Sosibios, third century (Clement, Censorinus)	1171
Ephoros, fourth century (Strabo, Clement)	1135

It must be recognised that numbers and numerals were very easily distorted in manuscript transmission, and cannot be accepted with confidence when they rest upon a single authority.

The variation of years, omitting the extravagant assumption of Douris, is 135, and their mean is 1203, very nearly the date given by the Parian chronicler. The methods by which these authorities obtained their results are seldom reported by the transmitters. Douris is also an exception here. Clement says that he placed the Fall of Troy a thousand years before the Crossing of Alexander from Europe to Asia (in 334 B.C.). Douris was a romantic historian of a modern kind who brought his characters to life by engaging them in dramatic conversations. His date had therefore no chronological significance, but it is interesting for the mystical application of the millennium to two great crises in the relations of Greece with Asia, and for the fact that a date so much above all others could be considered seriously by contemporary and later critics. His was not the only association of the millennium with the Fall.

Another was embodied in a strange tale about a religious penance imposed by the Delphic Oracle upon the people of Locris in expiation of the sin of the Locrian Aias, who had used violence of some kind to Cassandra in the temple of Athena at the sack of Troy. The only authority for all the details of the story is the Byzantine scholiast, John Tzetzes, on the iambic poem *Alexandra* (Cassandra) written by Lycophron in the third century B.C. The poet's obscure allusions are laboriously explained by his commentator:

The people of Locris, being afflicted with pestilence and famine because of the sin of Aias, were instructed by the god to propitiate Athena in Ilion for a thousand years by sending there two maidens selected by lot. When these were on their way the Trojans went to meet them and killed them if they caught them. They burnt their bones with wild and sterile wood and cast their ashes into the sea from Mount Traron in the Troad. Then the Locrians sent more girls. If any escaped they entered the temple of Athena secretly and became priestesses, sweeping and sprinkling the temple. But they did not approach the goddess or leave the temple except by night. They had their hair cut short, wore a single shift and went barefoot. The first of the Locrian maidens were Periboia and Cleopatra. At first the Locrians sent the girls, afterwards year-old infants with their nurses. When the thousand years had passed at the end of the Phocian War, they stopped this kind of sacrifice, as Timaios of Sicily says. Callimachos of Cyrene has also celebrated the story. Traron is a promontory of the Troad from which one of the Locrian maidens was thrown down. Lycophron says 'by night' because they did not enter the town in daylight but at night, since the Trojans were always waiting to kill them brutally. Rhoiteion was the place (at which the girls landed) in the Troad. The Trojans were ordered to go out against the girls with stones and swords when they knew that they were arriving from Locris, for so armed they received the maidens in order to kill them. The Trojans had a public ordinance commending those who killed them.

The Phocian War for control of the sanctuary at Delphi came to an end through the intervention of Philip of Macedon, father of Alexander, in 346 B.C., so that this estimate of the Fall of Troy would have been 1346, twelve years above that proposed by Douris. Timaios is not made responsible for the chronology by Tzetzes, nor could he have regarded it with approval, his own date for the Fall being 1193. Since he was an intolerant person, he may well have cited the Locrian belief as an example of popular stupidity. In any case, if he said that the penance had come to an end he was too hasty, for it is reported in several later testimonies to have gone on after that time. Aelian says that Antigonos of Macedon, at the end of the fourth century, directed the Locrian towns to decide by lot which of them should bear the burden, and Plutarch says that it had stopped not long before his time (first century A.D.) Strabo says that it did not begin before the Persian conquest of the Troad (sixth century B.C.)

The best evidence for the existence of the compulsory temple-service in the third century B.C. is provided by an inscription found in Locris in 1896. This prescribes the legal conditions upon which the clan of *Aianteioi* were to be relieved of certain political disabilities on condition that they made themselves responsible for the whole duty in future. The girls, according to Polybius, had formerly been selected by lot from noble families who were known as the Hundred Houses of Locris. The inscription contains no reference to any possible maltreatment of the girls, and implies that each pair came home after their year of service.

It is surprising that any modern scholars should represent the killing of the Locrian maidens as an established fact; less surprising, perhaps, that some of them should omit from the testimonies the manifestly false statement of the scholiast that some of these priestesses or temple-servants were babes-in-arms on their dangerous arrival at Troy. This has considerable bearing on the honesty and common sense of Byzantine scholarship. The origin of the statement is as obvious as its falsity. Classical authorities said that the service was yearly; the Greek word for yearly and yearling is the same (*eniausios*); the Byzantine compiler took it as applying to the age of the girls, and added his own gloss 'with their nurses'.

Lycophron did not invent the story of a strange rite on the girls' arrival in the Troad, though he may have added the blood-curdling details that he assigns appropriately to his demented prophetess:

> And every man of Ilion shall track
> The maidens, holding in his hand a stone
> Or sable sword or stout bull-slaying axe
> Or weighty branch of Phalacraian fir,
> Eager to sate his hand athirst for blood.
> The law shall not condemn, but grave the name
> And fame of him that kills the accursed race.

His is the only extant allegation of violence. Aeneas, who is known as Tacticus because he wrote on military tactics (in the century before Lycophron), refers only to attempted interception on the part of the Trojans. He cites their failure as illustrating the difficulty of stopping a well-planned convoy:

for the men at Ilion have not yet been able, even in that long time and with all their effort, to prevent the Locrian maidens from entering the city.

Apart from the dubious authority of Lycophron, the details of his story are incredible. If the Trojans had really tried to catch the girls on their five-mile journey from Rhoiteion to Troy, they would have done so. If any such practice had been current in the time of Herodotus he would surely have reported it when opportunity occurred, and he had the opportunity in describing the march of Xerxes from Sardis to Athens in the year 480. Xerxes stopped at Troy, where his army drank the Scamander dry, and went up to the Pergamon of Priam, since he had a great desire to see the place. When he had seen everything and enquired into all particulars, he made a sacrifice of a thousand oxen to the Trojan Athena, while the Magi poured libations to the heroes who had died at Troy.

The omission of Herodotus to mention any vindictive treatment of the temple-servants is the more significant in view of his description of an alleged rite of human sacrifice at a later moment in the march of Xerxes, at Halos in Thessaly. There he tells the story of a penalty which was still exacted in theory from the posterity of Phrixos, who rode to Colchis on the golden-fleeced ram before the voyage of the Argo.

Human sacrifice was a bogey which Greek writers paraded for occasional enjoyment of self-righteous horror. It was imputed to distant ancestors (Agamemnon at Aulis, Menelaos in Egypt, and others), and to contemporary members of the Hellenic family living in backward conditions or remote localities. Thucydides says that some of the Aitolians of his day were savages, if not cannibals; the author of the Platonic dialogue *Minos* accepts the tales of human sacrifice at Halos and in Arcadia; but there is no evidence of such barbarous practices in European or Asiatic Greece.

The historical Ilion was a miserable place until it was taken in hand to some extent by Alexander and his successors, and ultimately adopted as their Mother City by Julius Caesar and the Roman Emperors. The perennial ills of Ilion were proverbial. It was not a direct descendant of the Homeric city, although its Greek inhabitants would have it so, but a late foundation from Locris.

That is to say, the temple-maidens, daughters of the hundred First Families of mainland Locris, were received at Troy by their own relatives. The fact of a compulsory temple-service is established, and there is no reason to doubt that there was a popular celebration connected with the arrival of the girls. Stone-throwing, chases, bonfires, leaping from rocks and casting ashes into the sea were not infrequent practices in Greek religious ritual, and may in some instances have survived from primitive human sacrifice. In course of time their origins were forgotten, and mythical or historical explanations of them were invented. At Troizen there was a festival called the Stone-throwing (*Lithobolia*) in honour of Damia and Auxesia, of whom Pausanias reports: 'They say these girls came from Crete and were stoned to death by getting between two parties in a town riot'. Damia and Auxesia were, as their names denote, minor deities of growth and increase. They were worshipped as heroines in several localities, and the stone-throwing was part of the process of expelling noxious influences as scapegoats or otherwise for the protection of the crops. The same kind of mistaken ritual seems to have become attached to the arrival of the Locrian maidens. It is very likely that Cleopatra and Periboia, who are named by Tzetzes as the first two girls from Locris (a fact which nobody could have known), were really a pair of minor goddesses corresponding to Damia and Auxesia at Troizen and elsewhere, and that an aggressive demonstration was a relic of their cult at Troy.

Of the dates for the Fall of Troy that were proposed by reputable historians, most, if not all, were based upon the genealogies of the royal Lacedaimonian families, since the Return of the Heracleids was the event of primary interest for their authors. They were the most stable pedigrees that the Greeks possessed, though they were partly fictitious. Variations were admissible at several points: in the number of generations (whether the pedigree began with Aristodemos or one of his twin sons), in the number of years assumed for the generation (40, 33 or less), or in the length of the interval between the Return and the Fall of Troy.

The date quoted by Herodotus, which is one of the highest in the series (about 1250 B.C.) was evidently derived from the old 40-year generation. The lowest recorded estimate, that of Ephoros (1135 B.C.) is demonstrably based upon the 33-year generation without regard to fictitious regnal years. His date for the Return as transmitted by Clement is equivalent to 1069 B.C., that is 18 generations at three to a century (600 years) from the death of Pausanias, the Spartan regent and commander at Plataia, in the year 469. It is a reasonable assumption that he counted 66 years for the two generations to the Fall of Troy. Strabo says that the Return of the Heracleids was about 60 years after that event. The lowest date for the Return is that of Phainias of Eresos, 1049 B.C., 20 years later than Ephoros. He is said by Clement to have placed it 715 years before the Crossing of Alexander in 334, but his method of computation is not known.

Other authorities, as Sosibios and Eratosthenes, kept the regnal years or altered them slightly, and made their own adjustments at the point of contact of the king-lists with the Olympiads. The outstanding question is, why did Eratosthenes select for the Fall of Troy the period of 407 years before the First Olympiad? The answer seems to be that he took it from Ctesias.

Ctesias is described in a recent handbook of Greek literature as an amusing liar; but he was an unconscious humorist and his mendacity was beyond the reach of contemporary criticism. He was a Greek physician and surgeon, a citizen of Cnidos in Caria, who lived for some years (Diodorus says seventeen) at the Persian Court as the personal attendant of the king, Artaxerxes II. Xenophon says that he was present at the battle of Cunaxa (401 B.C.), where he dressed the wound that Cyrus dealt his brother, and afterwards wrote an account of the death of Cyrus from the Persian side. It was a rambling and inconclusive story, which Plutarch, giving a shortened version of it in his *Life of Artaxerxes*, compares with the process of hacking a man to death with a blunt sword. Plutarch distributes some uncomplimentary epithets in his references to Ctesias: long-winded, vain, melodramatic, self-seeking, mendacious. But Demetrius, writing *On Style* about the time of Plutarch, says that people who criticise the work of Ctesias adversely, fail to recognise the fact that he was really a poet.

Before the Macedonian and Roman conquests he was the only Greek source of information for Middle Asiatic affairs, and his known intimacy with the Court of Persia supported the authority that he claimed for his statements. Even Plutarch accepted it in matters of which Ctesias had personal experience and no apparent reason for invention. On his return to Greece at the beginning of the fourth century, he published, among many other things, a history of Persia in twenty-three books and one book on India. The first six books of the *Persica* covered the pre-Persian periods, and supplied most of the information that Diodorus reproduced in his histories of the Assyrians and Medes.

The original works of Ctesias are lost, but Photius made summaries of Books *vii* to *xxiii* of the *Persica* and of the whole of the *Indica*. That was a much less plausible work than the *Persica*, but it supplied the world with many of the fantastic stories, of dog-headed men and similar curiosities of the East, which persisted in medieval literature. Strabo says, on the authority of Nearchos, the commander of Alexander's ships, that Alexander himself was attracted to India by tales which could only have been those of Ctesias. Photius ends his summary of the *Indica* with a note on the author's methods which would have applied as well to the *Persica*:

In writing these fables Ctesias professes to tell the absolute truth. He insists that the things which he describes he has either seen himself or learned from eye-witnesses, and that he has omitted many greater marvels because he did not wish people without experience of the facts to think that he had made incredible statements.

The Persian Empire, which represented Asia to the Greeks when they first turned their attention to history, was a pattern for imaginative ideas of previous Oriental powers of which they knew little more than a few names and places. In this schematic history the region which Herodotus calls Upper Asia, that is to say the countries lying between the Anatolian river Halys and India, was controlled successively by single nations, Assyrians, Medes and Persians. Nothing was known of Hittites nor of their Anatolian dependencies or rivals. Each holder of the ideal hegemony inherited the credits and liabilities of its predecessor. Thus Herodotus makes the Persians claim that their attacks on Greece in the fifth century were reprisals for prehistoric Greek aggressions in the time of Assyrian domination, the abduction of Medeia from Colchis and the sack of Troy.

Ctesias recorded the fabulous origins of Nineveh and Babylon and the establishment of an Assyrian Empire, a Median revolt followed by the destruction of Nineveh and its sequel in a Median Empire, and the conquest of the Medes by the Persians. The historical facts are that the hegemony of Mesopotamia and parts of Western Asia was held alternately by Babylonians and Assyrians (whom ancient historians could not distinguish from each other) from the third millennium until the destruction of Nineveh by Babylonians and Medes in 612 B.C. The Median sovereignty passed to the Persians under Cyrus in the year 549, and Babylon was taken by Cyrus in 538. The beginnings of Babylonians and Assyrians and of their Sumerian and Elamite predecessors are still beyond the range of history.

Ctesias gave 33 kings and 1306 years to the Assyrians, 9 kings and 317 years to the Medes. Diodorus, following him, records the names of his nine Median kings with their regnal years:

ARBACES	28 years
MANDAUCAS	50
SOSARMOS	30
ARTYCAS	50
ARBANES	22
ARTAIOS	40
ARTYNES	22
ASTYBARAS	40
ASPADAS	(35)

Diodorus omits the years of the last king, Aspadas, but says that he was the person whom the Greeks called Astyages; Photius says that Ctesias called him Astyiagas. Since Herodotus assigns 35 years to Astyages and agrees with Ctesias in the years of his two predecessors, 35 can safely be supplied for Aspadas here. The total number of years in Ctesias was therefore 317. He made the mistake of equating the fall of Nineveh with the first year of the Median dynasty. Since Greek historians placed the accession of Cyrus wrongly in the first year of the Fifty-fifth Olympiad (560 B.C. instead of 549), the date of Ctesias for the fall of the Assyrian Empire is 877 B.C. in modern terms.

Diodorus, still citing Ctesias, says that the Assyrian dynasty lasted for 33 generations from Ninos, the fictitious eponym of Nineveh, to Sardanapallos, the degenerate Oriental monarch of Greek fable. Early Christian chronographers present emended lists of 36, 37, or 40 names which doubtless include the 33 of Ctesias, since most of their authorities cite him. The list of Eusebius is collated here with the chronology derived from Ctesias and some of the events that are now known to have occurred at particular times. The three names bracketed are among those omitted in the Armenian History of Moses of Chorene (sixth century A.D.)

Years B.C. by chronology of Ctesias	*Kings* *of the Assyrians* (from Eusebius)	*Historical Events*
		Empire of Sharru-kin (Sargon) of Agade, *c.* 2650. Conquests of Naram-sin, *c.*2500.
2183	1. NINUS 2. SEMIRAMIS 3. NINYAS	Empire of Hammurabi of Babylon.

	4.	ARIUS	Reign of Shamshi-adad in Assyria.
(2000)	5.	ARALIUS	Assyrian penetration of Anatolia.
	6.	XERXES	
	7.	ARMAMITHRES	Hittites raid Babylonia in reign of Samsu-ditana, *c.* 1900.
	8.	BELOCHUS	
	9.	BALAEUS	
(1800)	10.	ALTADAS	
	11.	MAMYTHUS	Kassite Dynasty at Babylon, *c.* 1750–1170.
	12.	MACCHALEUS	Rise of Assyria under Shamshi-adad II.
	13.	SPHAERUS	
	14.	MAMYLUS	
(1600)	15.	SPARAETHUS	Babylon sacked by Hittites under Mursil I.
	16.	ASCATADES	
	17.	AMYNTAS	
	18.	BELOCHUS	Babylonian and Assyrian rivalry.
	19.	BALATORES	
(1400)	20.	LAMPRIDES	Babylon controlled by Assyrians under Ashur-uballit II and Enlil-nirari.
	21.	SOSARES	
	22.	LAMPARES	
	23.	PANYAS	Assyrian conquests of Adad-nirari I and Shalmaneser I.
	24.	SOSARMUS	
1200)	25.	MITHRAEUS	Destruction of Hittite Empire.
1183	26.	TEUTAMUS (TEUTAEUS)	
	27.	THINAEUS	Kassites expelled and Pashê Dynasty founded at Babylon: Nebuchadrezzar I.
	28.	DERCYLUS	
	29.	EUPALMEUS (LAUOSTHENES)	Assyrian conquests of Tiglath-pileser I.
(1000)	30.	PERITIADES	
	31.	OPHRATAOUS (OPHRATANES)	
	32.	ACRAZANES	

877	33. SARDANAPALLUS '*Fall of Nineveh*' (according to Ctesias)	Assyrian Empire established by Ashur-nasir-pal II and Shalmaneser III, 884-824. Regency of Queen Sammuramat, 811-808. Revival of Babylon under Nabonassar, *c.* 745. Assyrian conquests of Tiglath-pileser III, 745-727. Capture of Damascus and Samaria, 732, 722. Sargonid Dynasty in Assyria, 722-612. Sargon in Cyprus and Cilicia, *c.* 710. Conquest of Egypt by Esarhaddon and Ashur-bani-pal ('Sardanapallus'), 671-663. Conquest of Elam by Ashur-bani-pal, 640. Chaldean Dynasty at Babylon: Nabopolassar, 625. Shin-shar-iskun last king of Assyria, 620. Nineveh destroyed by Babylonians and Medes, 612.

It is not worth while (as Diodorus might have said) to enquire into the Semitic, Anatolian or Persian names that may underlie these Greek hybrids. But it is worth noting, as an indication of its literary source, that the name of the twenty-sixth king, Teutamos, occurs in the *Iliad* as that of the grandfather of two of the Pelasgians in the Trojan *Catalogue*.

The chronology of Ctesias is delivered thus in one manuscript passage of Diodorus: 'Under Sardanapallos the empire of the

Assyrians fell to the Medes, having lasted more than thirteen hundred years, *plus* sixty.' Recent editors delete '*plus* 60' on the analogy of another passage of Diodorus: 'So the empire of the Assyrians, which had lasted more than 1300 years, was destroyed by the Medes, as has been said above.' That is doubtless what Diodorus wrote, for he had a way of reducing precise figures to round numbers. '*Plus* 60' in the first passage is evidently a manuscript corruption of '*plus* 6', a marginal gloss by some commentator which made its way into the text. There is ample evidence to show that Ctesias wrote '1306'. Georgius Syncellus (ninth century A.D.) and Agathias (sixth century) attribute that number explicitly to him. Since his date for the fall of Nineveh, in modern terms, is 877 B.C., his date for the beginning of the Assyrian dynasty is equivalent to 2183.

Ninos, the eponym and reputed founder of Nineveh, was said to have had predecessors on the Assyrian throne, notably Belos (Bel–Marduk of Babylon). Babylon was said to have been built by Semiramis, the wife of Ninos. He was represented as the organiser of Assyrian military power and conqueror of the Oriental world from the Indus to the Nile, but the only military exploits that Ctesias attributed to her alone were the extension of the Egyptian conquest to Ethiopia and Libya and an unsuccessful attempt to invade India.

These fables of pretended Oriental conquerors were adopted by the Greeks from Babylonian and Egyptian sources. The Egyptian counterpart of Ninos was Sesostris, but his name at least was historical, being a Greek version of the three Senusrets of the Twelfth Dynasty. An Assyrian queen whose name came near to Semiramis was Sammu-ramat, widow of Shamshi-adad and regent for Adad-nirari III at the end of the ninth century.

Diodorus sums up his Assyrian history as follows:

There was no need to write all the names of the kings and the number of years in the reign of each, because they did not do anything worth mentioning. The only considerable event was the expedition sent by the Assyrians in aid of the Trojans, which was led by Memnon son of Tithonos. When Teutamos was king of Asia, being twentieth from Ninyas son of Semiramis, it is said that the Greeks made their attack on Troy with Agamemnon, when the Assyrians had held the hegemony of Asia for more than a thousand years. That Priam, hard pressed by the war and as king of the Troad being subject to the king of Assyria, sent envoys to him for assistance; that Teutamos despatched ten thousand Ethiopians and as many Susians with two hundred chariots and Memnon son of Tithonos in command. He was much admired for his bravery and killed many Greeks in battle, but was ultimately caught and killed by the Thessalians. The Ethiopians recovered and burnt his body and took his ashes back to Tithonos. This is the account of Memnon which the natives say is recorded in the royal documents.

Ctesias was not likely to acquire authentic Assyrian information at Susa or any other residence of the Persian king. Prehistoric peoples did not preserve native traditions of aliens with whom their own relations had been hostile; their memories of such predecessors could hardly go back beyond the points of contact. If Ctesias had had interest or opportunity enough to consult the temple-scribes at Babylon, as Herodotus did, his story of the Assyrian Empire might have had some historical content. As it was, he had no knowledge of any events in Babylonia or Assyria before the Median conquest. The real Assyrian Empire was in fact beginning its impressive history at the moment to which Ctesias assigned its end.

The royal documents from which he said his information about Memnon was taken are more precisely described by Diodorus in relation to his history of the Median kings. They were:

Parchments (*diphtherai*) in which the Persians keep the record of ancient events as by law ordained, and which Ctesias had himself studied in detail in publishing his history for Greek readers.

It may be desirable even now to examine the realities of these Ctesian documents. If Medes and Persians had possessed contemporary written records of their early kings, those would not have been manuscripts on parchment. The form of writing used in Western Asia at that time for royal archives was the cuneiform script, which was designed to be impressed or engraved.

The regular official archives were tablets and cylinders of clay. An Assyrian tablet dated in the sixth year of Sargon (715 B.C.) records his deportation to Syria of a Median chief, Daiokku, who had the same name, if he was not the same person, as the first Median king of Herodotus, Deioces, corresponding to the Artaios of Ctesias. It is not likely that Daiokku had reason or opportunity to commemorate his own contacts with Assyria, still less likely that the Persians kept any written records at that time. The earliest Persian document that has yet been found is a gold tablet inscribed in cuneiform with the name and title of Ariyaramna (Ariamnes), grandson of Hakhamanish, the founder of the Achaimenian dynasty. Its date is about 600 B.C.

The historical Persian manuscripts that Ctesias would have known were written in Aramaic script on parchment or papyrus. If he had even seen the earlier documents which he claimed to have studied, he could not have described them as parchments, nor could he or his informants have read them. Their knowledge or ignorance of the cuneiform script and Persian history is revealed in his account of one of the achievements of Semiramis:

When Semiramis had finished her constructional works she made an expedition against Media with a large force. When she came to the mountain which is called Bagistanos, she encamped near by and laid out a park. The Bagistanos mountain is sacred to Zeus. On the side against the park it has sheer precipices rising to a height of seventeen stades (11,000 feet). She smoothed off the lowest part and cut on it a portrait of herself attended by a hundred spearmen, and on the rock she cut an inscription in Syrian letters saying that Semiramis scaled the aforesaid precipice and reached the summit from the plain below by piling up the pack-saddles of the transport animals in her train.

Ctesias placed Semiramis about 2150 B.C. Her rock-cut memorial is the great monument at Bisutun carved and inscribed by the

Persian king Dareios I to commemorate his final establishment of the Achaimenian dynasty in and after the year 521.

The monument of Behistun, as it is usually called, is cut on a precipitous mountain-spur, five hundred feet above the ground, on the ancient road from Babylon to Ecbatana. It is nearly sixty feet long, and consists of a sculptured panel, eighteen feet long and ten feet high, flanked by cuneiform inscriptions in three languages, Persian, Elamite and Babylonian. The central relief represents Dareios with two Persian officers receiving eight leaders of the reconquered provinces, whose necks are roped together and arms tied behind their backs. Dareios sets his foot on the chief rebel, Gaumata (the Pseudo-Smerdis of Herodotus), who lies supine. A tenth captive, named as Skunka, was inserted at a later date to celebrate a Scythian victory of Dareios (Plate 3).

The inscriptions record the royal lineage of Dareios and his recovery of the several kingdoms which had revolted after the death of Cambyses and the impersonation of his brother by the Magus Gaumata, in the course of which Dareios says that he fought nineteen battles and captured nine kings. It is hard to believe that even Ctesias could have misrepresented the sculptured figures so grossly if he had ever seen them, but it is evident that his Persian informants, officers of the court with whom he lived for many years and who must have known the monument, were equally ignorant of its significance. Yet it was the most impressive as well as the most important document in Persian history, and the events which it commemorated were only a hundred years before their time. There is an ironical comment on the shortness of ancient memories in the solemn injunction that Dareios reiterates in the inscriptions:

Saith Daryavaush the King: If thou shalt behold this inscription and these sculptures and shalt not destroy them but shalt preserve them as long as thy line endureth, then may Auramazda be thy friend and may thy house be numerous.

The only exception made by Diodorus to his statement that no event worth mentioning occurred between the reigns of Semiramis and Sardanapallos was the Trojan War, which Ctesias placed in the time of the twenty-sixth king, Teutamos: Diodorus calls him the twentieth from Ninyas son of Semiramis. Diodorus puts the war at a time when the Assyrians had held the hegemony of Asia for more than a thousand years. Ctesias may or may not have written 'more than' a thousand, but the specious precision of his Assyrian chronology, and Plutarch's report of his romantic tendencies, suggest that having introduced the millennium dramatically, as Douris and the Locrians did, he would not have spoilt its effect with qualifications. If the qualification came from Diodorus, he may have had in mind the uncertain beginnings of the Assyrian dynasty in Belos and other predecessors of Ninos, whom he recognised as kings. In any case, the date more or less precisely indicated by Ctesias for the Trojan War was 623 years (1306 for the Assyrians + 317 for the Medes — 1000 for Troy) before the supposed accession of Cyrus at the Fifty-fifth Olympiad (560 B.C.): that is to say 1183 B.C., or 407 years before the First Olympiad. It cannot be an accidental coincidence that this was the interval adopted by Eratosthenes for his Fall of Troy.

An Alexandrian scholar would not have been less critical than Plutarch of the ignorance and pretence of Ctesias, but like Plutarch and others, Eratosthenes could accept statements that seemed to stand upon documentary evidence. The story of Memnon's expedition to Troy was one of these. The assurance of Ctesias that his Asiatic informants had found the facts in the royal records was accepted by his Greek contemporaries, who believed in the reality of the Trojan War and the existence of Memnon, and were neither qualified nor disposed to criticise the evidence. The process bears a remarkable similarity to that by which some modern scholars have welcomed speculative identifications of legendary Greek and Trojan personages in Hittite cuneiform texts. The story was plausible enough for Plato to repeat in his *Laws*:

The people who lived at Ilion at that time were moved by reliance on the power of Assyria, which had grown up about Ninos, to venture upon the Trojan War, for much of the organisation of that empire had survived. The capture of Troy took place as a second grave offence on the part of the Greeks, since Troy belonged to the Assyrian Empire.

The *Persica* of Ctesias was a recent publication when Plato wrote.

Some later historians embroidered the Memnon legend in the style of Ctesias. Eusebius quotes the text of a letter which Priam addressed to Teutamos in his emergency and cites Cephalion as his authority for it:

An army of Greeks has invaded your country and attacked me. We have met them in battle, sometimes we are victorious, sometimes defeated. The present position is that Hector has been killed, and so have many other brave sons of mine. Send therefore troops to help us and a valiant commander.

Two Greek writers used the name of Cephalion, both apparently with some fraudulent intent, and were so far successful in obscuring their identities that Suidas has made them into one. He says that Cephalion or Cephalon of Gergithos wrote histories in the Ionic dialect in the time of Hadrian. This was evidently the author from whom Eusebius took Priam's letter. Photius treats him less respectfully, and says that he suppressed his name in imitation of Homer. But he seems to have impersonated an earlier Cephalion, who is said by Dionysius (writing long before the time of Hadrian) to have been a very old historian. Athenaeus quotes from a work *Troica* bearing his name, and cites one Hegesianax of Alexandria as its author. The best known town of Gergithos was in the Troad; Strabo says there was a place in Aiolis called Gergithes, to which Cephalion belonged, but Herodotus says casually that the Gergithai of the Troad were a remnant of the ancient Teucrians. The Gergithian Cephalion was evidently put forward as a possessor of authentic information about the Trojan war, and Hegesianax, if Athenaeus was right, would be the first recorded Homeric impostor and the only one whose real name is known.

The canonical date for the Fall of Troy, 1183 B.C., was immediately adopted from these inventions and the false assurances attached to them by their authors. There is a final question: how did Ctesias arrive at it? The date itself was not far from the mean of current computations, and could therefore be acceptable to historians. The fact that it was a thousand years below his fictitious date for Ninos may have been fortuitous, or he may have fixed upon a plausible date for Troy and placed Ninos a thousand years above it. His own contributions were the mystical millenium and the false historical authority.

The ancient dates for the Fall of Troy (except that of Douris) are thus seen to be a single point in time presented with arithmetical variations: two conjectural generations before the traditional Return of the Heracleids. Since they covered a period of more than 135 years, some of them ought to have approached the real date closely; but we have not yet any means of determining which those may be. Archaeological discovery can define successive buildings, destructions and rebuildings of Mycenae and Troy, but cannot identify the builders or destroyers with precision. Contemporary written references, the only reliable source of information, are not yet available for this epoch. They may still be found in Hittite texts, or in those of Western Anatolian kingdoms, or even in Mycenean texts in Greece. Assyria, Babylonia and Egypt were too far removed from Aegean interests to have particular knowledge of a Trojan city.

There are however three entries in Egyptian records which describe historical conditions like those represented by Homer, and may contain names of some of the Aegean peoples who were active about the time of the Trojan War. It must be noted that foreign names are written syllabically and without vocalisation in Egyptian hieroglyphs, so that unless the names are known from other sources the vowels cannot be added with assurance. Thus the name that has been reproduced as Akaiwasha and equated with Akhaivoi appears in the Egyptian script as K-W-SH. It is vocalised formally now as *Ekwesh*, and cannot be elaborated beyond that point without external evidence.

The relevant records are (in Breasted's translations):

5　The Philistine invasion of Syria, 1190 B.C. The *Peleset* warriors have feather-crowned helmets; their women and children are in the ox-carts. The men with horned and ball-crested helmets are *Shardina*, Egyptian mercenaries. Detail of wall-sculpture in the Mortuary Temple of Rameses III at Medinet Habu, Thebes.

6 (*Above*) Hittite sphinx. Basalt relief from the Herald's Wall at Carchemish, about 900 B.C. (*Below*) A decorative Greek version of the same monster, from a Protocorinthian oil-bottle, about 650 B.C.

1. Several versions of the victory claimed by Rameses II in the battle which he fought in his fifth year (about 1288 B.C.) against the Hittite King Mursil II at Kadesh in North Syria. The fullest pictorial record is on the walls of the temple of Amon at Karnak; the longest literary account is the poem that goes by the name of Pentaur, the scribe of one of the extant manuscripts. Among the contingents named in these texts as serving with the Hittite forces are *Derden, Pedes, Kelekesh, Mesa* and *Luka*. They may have been Dardanians, Pedasians, Cilicians, Mysians and Lycians, all of whom are known from Homeric or later Greek references as belonging to western Anatolia. If the identification of Dardanians and Pedasians is correct, it may mean that the Dardanian city of Troy and Pedasos in the Troad had not then been destroyed.

2. An inscription of Mernepthah on the wall of the temple of Amon at Karnak celebrating the defeat in his fifth year (about 1225 B.C.) of a concerted attack on the western Delta by Libyans in alliance with 'northerners coming from all lands'. They are specified as *Teresh, Shekelesh, Sherden, Luka,* and *'Ekwesh* of the countries of the sea'. Sherden (or Shardina) and Luka (or Lykki) are known at the beginning of the fourteenth century from references in the Amarna Letters (foreign correspondence of Amenhotep IV), the Lykki as raiders of the Syrian coast, the Shardina as mercenary soldiers in Egyptian service. The Luka were doubtless Lycians; the Shardina were certainly foreigners from oversea and are often represented in Egyptian pictorial reliefs, but their place of origin is not known. Obvious speculations have connected them with Sardis and Sardinia, but though they may ultimately have given its name to the Italian island, they can hardly have come from there to Egypt, either as auxiliaries in the fourteenth century or as adversaries in this record. The Teresh have been similarly identified as Etruscans.

The equation of Ekwesh with Akhaivoi is more plausible. The last syllable *-esh* or *-sha*, which occurs in most of these names, appears to be a tribal suffix used by the Egyptians in describing foreigners, and may be removed. The Egyptian *K* is not phonetically equivalent to the Greek *KH*, but such inaccuracy is possible in transference from an unfamiliar language; the vocalisation presents less difficulty since the vowels are not expressed in the hieroglyphic script.

3.   The third record is best preserved in inscriptions and reliefs on the walls of the mortuary temple of Rameses III at Medinet Habu. The western Delta was attacked in his fifth year (about 1200 B.C.) by Libyans, as in Mernepthah's reign, allied with peoples of the sea, again described as northerners but named as *Peleset* and *Thekel*, 'who devastate the land. They are warriors upon the land, also on the sea.'

A more dangerous attack in Rameses' eighth year came down the Syrian coast, where he advanced to meet it. This movement was a massed migration by sea and land: the pictorial reliefs show the ships in battle, with Shardina fighting on both sides, and the families and goods of the invaders carried in wagons on the shore (Plate 5). The principal text reads:

The northerners in their isles were disturbed. Not one stood before their hands, from Kheta (Hittites), Kode, Carchemish, Arvad, Alasa they were wasted. They came with fire prepared before them forward to Egypt. Their main support was Peleset, Thekel, Shekelesh, Denyen, Weshesh. These lands were united, and they laid their hands upon the land as far as the circle of the earth. Their hearts were confident, full of their plans.

This is an explicit record of the fall of the Hittite Empire. Most of the migrants would have been fugitives escaping from the new Anatolian raiders, but some, as the *Peleset* and *Thekel*, who took part in the previous Libyan attack, seem to have been raiders themselves. Rameses prevented them from reaching Egypt, but their defeat cannot have been so destructive as he represented, for the *Peleset*, afterwards known as the Philistines, effected a permanent settlement in the south and gave their name to Palestine. The *Denyen* have been thought to be the Danaoi of Homer, but they are mentioned as *Danauna* in the Amarna Letters in relation to North Syria. They may have belonged to the south of Asia Minor, where the city of Adana seems to have preserved their name.

The record of Mernepthah represents the *Ekwesh* as one of the predatory peoples from the northern sea who began to disturb the peace of the Nile Delta in piratical attacks at the end of the thirteenth century. That is the other side of the picture presented in the *Odyssey*, where Odysseus describes his own imaginary raid, which ended badly, and in the *Iliad*, where attacks on Troy are represented as a nine years siege. Archaeological evidence shows that commercial relations of Greece with Egypt, which had been regular until that time, were broken off at the end of the thirteenth century and were not directly resumed before the eighth century. Taken in conjunction with the Egyptian statements of disorder in the Aegean world about the year 1200, this fact supports the identification of *Ekwesh* with Achaians.

Possible Hittite references to Achaians, in cuneiform texts on clay tablets from Boghazkoï, are not yet more than conjectural equations of personal and local names. Some of them (as Attarissiyas = Atreus, and Tawagalawas = Eteocles or Deucalion) are too fantastic to consider seriously; but the Hittites must have been in contact with prehistoric Greeks in some coastal districts of Asia Minor, and their name for a Western Anatolian kingdom, Ahhiya or Ahhiyawa, may have been connected with Achaian establishments in the Aegean islands, the Cyclades or Rhodes, or on the Anatolian shores, or in Cyprus. Such settlements are known to have existed, and the significance of Hittite references to them would be chronological.

Ahhiyawa is first mentioned in records dating from 1350 to 1300 B.C., when its relations with the Hittite Empire were close and friendly. With the beginning of the thirteenth century the kings of Ahhiyawa became aggressive, and in the second half of the century one Attarissiyas was definitely hostile, but he seems to have operated inland in Anatolia. The records end with the Hittite Empire about 1200. There is not yet any reason beyond the resemblance in the place-name to connect the people of Ahhiyawa with the Achaians of Greece.

The sudden change of front in Mycenean relations with Egypt implies the dominance in Greece of a people who knew not Pharaoh nor anything of peaceful commerce. Its date at the end of the thirteenth century agrees with what is known on the Greek side about the introduction of a new cultural element marked by the funeral rite of cremation, which was Achaian but not Mycenean. Successful attacks by these people on the north-east shores of the Aegean are not likely to have been earlier than their establishment in Greece. The most favourable conditions for them would have developed after the destruction of the Hittite Empire. That Hittite influence had extended as far as the Aegean coast is proved by the rock-cut figures which Herodotus saw near Smyrna and Ephesos (Plate 4). An Achaian sack of Troy as represented by Homer might have taken place shortly before the end of the thirteenth century or at any moment within the next hundred years or so.

It has often been pointed out, but does not seem to be generally recognised, that the Achaians of Homer were not the same kind of people as the Myceneans who assimilated the high material culture of Crete in the sixteenth and fifteenth centuries B.C. The artistic vigour of that culture was declining naturally in the fourteenth century, but there is no material evidence of political or social change at that time. The people of Greece whom we call Myceneans lived in urban communities whose prosperity was based upon agriculture and maritime commerce with Syria and Egypt. We do not know what they called themselves, but there is no authority for extending the Achaian name to them. Homer's Achaians have a tribal organisation, so far as they have any. They are controlled by local chieftains loosely bound by military allegiance to a national king. Odysseus defines the Achaian name and nature in his first conversation with the Cyclops:

We are wandering Achaians making our way home from Troy, people of Agamemnon son of Atreus whose fame is now mightiest under the skies, for he sacked a great city and killed many people. But we come as suppliants to you, in the expectation that you will give us entertainment or some other gift that strangers are entitled to receive.

The men whom Odysseus had with him are described in the *Catalogue of Ships* and elsewhere in the *Iliad* as Cephallenes from Ithaca and other western islands. That was a tribal appellation like Hellenes; the island afterwards known as Cephallenia is not mentioned by Homer with that name. Achilles' men were Myrmidones from the northern province that was afterwards called Achaia; his old friend and neighbour Phoinix was chief of the Dolopes. When the tribes were settled in Mycenean cities they took local names, as Pylioi and Argeioi. Argos, with the fortresses of Mycenai and Tiryns in its plain, was the oldest and most powerful Mycenean centre, and its name was used to denote the Peloponnese or perhaps the whole of Achaian Greece, Argeioi being a geographical equivalent of Achaioi. The third Homeric name for the Greeks as a whole, Danaoi, seems, like Achaioi, to be tribal. It was attached in legend to the Argolid.

The ordinary means of acquiring wealth in the *Iliad* and *Odyssey* are by accepting or exacting valuable gifts from friends or strangers, thievery and piracy. Many of the works described in the poems had been procured by dishonesty or violence. The handsome lyre on which Achilles accompanied his own songs at Troy was loot from the city of Eëtion, the father of Andromache. The Mycenean boar-tusk cap which Meriones lent to Odysseus for his midnight raid had a long and discreditable pedigree:

On his head he put a cap of hide, which was stiffened on the inside with many straps of leather, and on the outside were white teeth of a fierce-tusked boar set thickly this way and that, and it was lined with felt. Autolycos took it long ago by burglary from the strong house of Amyntor son of Ormenos, gave it to Amphidamas of Cythera to take to Scandeia, Amphidamas gave it to Molos as a friendly gift, Molos gave it to his son Meriones to wear.

Boars' teeth pierced for attachment have been found in Mycenean tombs of the fifteenth century, and the helmet itself is represented in several ivory carvings. Autolycos was the maternal grandfather of Odysseus, and is celebrated in the *Odyssey* as the person 'who excelled all men in thievery and perjury', social accomplishments which he had acquired by grace of the god Hermes.

Achaian political conditions are reflected in Menelaos' invitation to Odysseus to leave his island outpost and come and live with him in a more civilised place:

I would have given him a city in Argos and built him a house, bringing him from Ithaca with his goods and his son and all his men, and driving out the people of one of the cities that lie round about and are subject to me their king.

It is evident that the Achaians were enjoying the remains of a civilisation which was not their own. The only contribution that they appear to have made to the amenities of life was cremation of the dead.

Homer's Achaian pedigrees do not go back beyond the grand-fathers of the men who fought at Troy, but that may be because he had no occasion to mention their earlier histories. In one instance, however, he (or some other poet) defines the origin of an Achaian family, and that the most important of them. The divine sceptre that gave Agamemnon his supreme power was given by Hermes to Pelops:

Pelops gave it to Atreus, shepherd of the people, Atreus at his death left it to Thyestes, rich in flocks, and Thyestes left it to Agamemnon to bear, that so he should be king of many islands and all Argos.

Argos in these passages is the Peloponnese, to which Pelops was said to have given its name. It is more likely to have received the name from a real or imaginary tribe of Pelopes, of which Pelops was the symbolical eponym. But his generation may stand, and also that of Thyestes, though he was represented by later genealogists as the brother and not the son of Atreus. That makes at most four generations, not more than a hundred and fifty years from the foundation of the dynasty to the Trojan War, or perhaps not more than a hundred, according to the Homeric legend.

5

MYTHICAL ASIATICS

Greeks and Asiatics – the Trojan 'Catalogue' – Lycian pedigrees – Bellero-
phon and Pegasos – the Chimaira – Anatolian earth-fires – Sarpedon and
Minos – ethnographical and etymological myth – the Aiolids – Homeric genea-
logies – Ethiopians – Memnon in Asia and Egypt – Tithonos – Didun and
Dido – the Amazons – Scythians and Mongols – hero worship.

Greek legends reveal no knowledge or memories of the Hittites.
The *Catalogue* of Trojan forces in the *Iliad* extends along the Black
Sea coast as far as the Hittite country (the unknown Halizones
and Alybê, 'the birthplace of silver', must be related to the river
Halys), but it makes no reference to the powerful empire that was
centred there in the fourteenth and thirteenth centuries, nor to the
kingdoms associated with it in western Anatolia, Asuwa, Arzawa,
Ahhiyawa, or others. This document cannot therefore be an
Achaian record, but must be an Aiolic or Ionian reconstruction of
native conditions at the time of the Hellenic colonisation.

The colonists were more mixed with the natives than their
heroic pedigrees would imply, and the natives shared the pedigrees with them. Herodotus says that the kings of some Ionian
cities were Codrids from Pylos (that is to say, descendants of Nestor), or Lycians of the blood of Glaucos son of Hippolochos. This
Glaucos was a leading ally of the Trojans in the *Iliad*, a grandson
of Bellerophon and so an Aiolid of Corinth. Herodotus also says
that the Ionians who claimed the best right to that name as emi-
grants from Athens had married Carian women whose husbands
and brothers they had killed, and that the women had bound
themselves by oath never to sit at meals with the men nor call
them by their names. He implies that this was an Ionian peculiar-
ity in his time; if so, it was an Oriental custom adopted by the

colonists and adjusted to Hellenic ideas by means of this historical fable.

The Dorian foundation of Halicarnassos was controlled in historical times by Carian dynasts, among whom two queens bearing the Greek name of Artemisia were particularly distinguished, the first by her disingenuous tactics at the battle of Salamis, the second by the world-famous tomb which she built for her husband Maussolos. Herodotus himself seems to have been at least half Carian, for his uncle Panyassis, who was one of the last poets to write what he would have called history in the old epic style, had a wholly Carian name.

The Ionians were therefore naturally disposed to cultivate an artificial Trojan legend, for it cannot be believed that Achaian raiders, even if their attacks extended over ten years or more, would have acquired or wished to acquire the intimate personal knowledge of their adversaries that is displayed in the *Iliad*. The characters, pedigrees, domiciles and domestic affairs of the Trojans and their allies must be inventions of Greek poets.

Ten Anatolian tribes or nations are cited in the Trojan *Catalogue*, but only three find more than casual mention in the narrative, Trojans, Dardanians and Lycians. The first two are one people, the Trojans being a Dardanian tribe: Tros in the Homeric genealogy was grandson of Dardanos. Trojans and Lycians are called upon by Hector in moments of stress as if there were no other allies in the field. Yet the Lycians of the *Catalogue* come from the historical Lycia, identified by its river Xanthos, at the southern extremity of Asia Minor: a rugged and inhospitable land and a most unlikely region to send an expeditionary force to Troy in the extreme north. 'Sarpedon and Glaucos were leaders of the Lycians, from Lycia far away, from eddying Xanthos'. It seems therefore that if there were Lycians in the prehistoric epos, they were not those of the Homeric *Catalogue* or of Greek history: the latter in fact called themselves Termilai. The Lycian name was probably used in Achaian times as a general term for people of the Anatolian coastlands. They were doubtless the *Luka* or *Lykki* who are named in

Egyptian records as raiding Syrian and Egyptian shores from the fourteenth to the twelfth century.

The pedigree of the Lycian leaders was recited on the battlefield by Glaucos at his famous meeting with Diomedes of Argos. He states that he and Sarpedon are grandsons of Bellerophon, Sarpedon's father being Zeus. Then he tells at length the story of Bellerophon, his Corinthian origin, his expulsion from Greece at the instance of the wicked wife of Proitos, king of Argos, who sent him to his Lycian father-in-law bearing his own death-warrant (the only Homeric mention of writing, if this whole episode is Homer's). The Lycian king sent him, as he thought, to his death against the Chimaira, the Solymoi, and the Amazons, and finally waylaid him with Lycian assassins, all of whom he slew. 'So when the king saw that he was the son of a god, he kept him there, gave him his daughter and half of his kingdom' in the true vein of popular romance. Thus Diomedes recognises Glaucos as a grandson of his own father's friend, without much regard for chronology, and they celebrate their meeting by an exchange of armour, upon which the poet makes the characteristically Hellenic comment that 'Zeus robbed Glaucos of his wits, since he gave away his golden armour for the bronze of Diomedes, the worth of a hundred oxen for the worth of nine'.

The Greek part of his pedigree was thus delivered by the Lycian Glaucos:

There is a city Ephyrê (Corinth) in the heart of horse-pasturing Argos, where Sisyphos dwelt, the craftiest of men, Sisyphos son of Aiolos; he had a son Glaucos, and his son was peerless Bellerophon.

Aiolos, Sisyphos and this first Glaucos were figures of Hellenic ethnographical and religious myth, but Bellerophon was a personage in Anatolian religion. His name was not Greek, and ancient etymologists could do no more with it than make him the slayer of an imaginary Belleros. Homer, or the author of this episode, describes the Chimaira cautiously, excusing its supernatural character by its divine origin. He says nothing about the winged horse, Pegasos, who was at least the means by which the monster was destroyed, but could not plausibly be associated with the narrator's grandfather. Homer's Chimaira was a lion in front, a snake behind, and a goat in the middle, and she breathed out raging fire. Hesiod's was more precisely marvellous:

A creature terrible and huge and swift and strong; she had three heads, one of a roaring lion, one of a goat, one of a snake, a mighty dragon, and she breathed out raging fire. She was slain by Pegasos and bold Bellerophon.

Monsters combining animal and human forms of many kinds are represented in the earliest Mesopotamian documents and were adopted by the Hittites. They were introduced into prehistoric Greece in comparatively simple shapes of griffins, sphinxes and winged horses, but all such motives disappeared in the atrophy of decorative art that followed the Achaian isolation of Greece and the Dorian invasion. They began to reappear with the renewal of Oriental contacts in the ninth century. A lion with a man's head set in the middle of its back in a Protocorinthian vase-painting of the seventh century is a decorative Greek version of the scheme presented by the sphinx with two heads at Carchemish; but this Hittite head wears the horned helmet of a god (Plate 6).

It is possible that the symbol of a winged horse had survived in the region of Corinth and attracted the cult of Bellerophon which was established there in historical times; but it is probable that the Aiolid ancestry devised by Ionian genealogists for their Lycian kings brought the heavenly horse as well as the hero to Corinth. Pegasos, like Bellerophon, had a name that was not Greek. Hesiod says that his father was Poseidon, his mother the Gorgon Medousa, and that Pegasos and a god in human form, Chrysaor, sprang from her neck when she was decapitated by Perseus. 'Pegasos flew away, leaving the earth, and went to the immortals; he lives in the halls of Zeus and bears the thunder and lightning for him.' The twin brother, Chrysaor (Golden Sword), is an appropriate personification of lightning, and was identified with Zeus

and with Bellerophon. There were cults of Zeus Chrysaor in Anatolia, and the name replaced Bellerophon's in a Carian version of
the pedigree. Another Homeric reference makes the Chimaira
Carian: she was 'bred by king Amisodaros to be the bane of
many men'.

Fire-breathing monsters are associated with lightning-gods on
Babylonian and Assyrian cylinder seals: they support the gods and
were doubtless meant to reinforce their powers. A rational Greek
view of this Oriental symbolism could see the animals as subjected
to the deities who stand upon them: the flaming breath enhances
the terror of the monster and the valour of the god. Pegasos and
the Chimaira became attractive subjects for Greek artistic ingenuity, but the Chimaira was never located in Greece; she lived
and died in Anatolia, in oil-bearing or volcanic regions where
earth-fires existed. The best-known of these in ancient times was
the flame of natural gas on a mountain near the sea in eastern
Lycia, between the cities of Phaselis and Olympos. Its Turkish
name is Yanar-Tash, the Fire Rock. Modern knowledge of the
place began with a casual observation from H.M.S. *Frederikssteen*,
Captain Francis Beaumont, F.R.S., when the ship lay off the Kara-
manian coast in July, 1811. There was seen at night a small but
steady light among the hills, which the captain, landing next day
to investigate, found to be a quietly burning flame of natural gas
about two feet across. He was told by the guide that shepherds
often cooked their food by it, but it was well known that the
Yanar would not roast meat that had been stolen.

Ctesias compared this fire with his imaginary Indian marvels,
adding the characteristic statement that it could be put out with
brushwood but not with water: a statement duly repeated by later
authorities. Pliny and others call the place Chimaira Mountain.

Homer's mention of Amisodaros as the monster's keeper gives
it a Carian habitat, and Strabo, who knew central Anatolia well,
describes several places where dangerous earth-fires were prev-
alent. He says that the upper Maeander valley was undermined
with fire and water, and around Mount Argaios in eastern Ana-

tolia, now an extinct volcano, the plain was riddled with fire-holes, 'perilous for most creatures and particularly for cattle, which fall into the hidden pits'. His testimony explains how the Chimaira came to be regarded by Asiatic Greeks as an embodiment of these alarming phenomena. Apollodorus says that it wasted the country and ravaged the cattle. The Homeric *Hymn to Pythian Apollo* says the same thing about the Python, the monstrous snake that infested Delphi. 'She did much harm to mortal men, much to their long-legged sheep.' At Delphi there was no fire in historical times but only the awful chasm of the Phaidriades, where anything might lurk, and the cleft which was said to exhale intoxicating vapour for the prophetess. The world-wide theme of terrestrial monsters destroyed by celestial gods was put to different uses in these two places: Apollo's destruction of the Python became a religious myth, Bellerophon's conquest of the Chimaira was worked into a secular legend, and the Anatolian lightning-god was transported to Greece as a Corinthian hero.

The name of the other Lycian leader in the *Iliad*, Sarpedon, the cousin of Glaucos, was also not Greek, and seems to have been, like that of their grandfather Bellerophon, at least the title of an Anatolian deity. It was a place-name in historical times, belonging to rocky headlands on the eastern Aegean coasts from Thrace in the north to Cilicia in the south, and was given in myth to the island where the Gorgons lived. There were cults of Apollo Sarpedonios and Artemis Sarpedonia in Cilicia, where the oracular functions of Artemis were inherited by Saint Thecla, the virgin disciple of Saint Paul.

Homer makes much of his Sarpedon's parentage as a son of Zeus by the daughter of Bellerophon. He was killed by Patroclos after his father had made elaborate provision for the rescue of his body by Apollo, its conveyance to Lycia by Sleep and Death, and its entombment there in native fashion. But there was another Lycian Sarpedon, also a son of Zeus, a brother of Minos of Crete. Homer does not mention him, and indeed he seems to have been added to the family of Europa as an ethnographical speculation.

Hesiod records his birth and his reign in Lycia, and doubtless told the story of his departure from Crete. In later writers it was connected with a prehistoric founding of Carian Miletos by a Cretan youth of that name over whom the brothers quarrelled: Sarpedon followed him and became king in Lycia. Two Lycian Sarpedons, both sons of Zeus, were properly regarded as one and the same person; but when the genealogists came to correlate the stories which the poets had elaborated, they found that the chronology was wrong. The first Sarpedon was a brother of Minos the grandfather of Idomeneus, who was grey-headed when he fought at Troy, where the second Sarpedon was killed. In the case of Minos the chronological discrepancy was removed by making two persons of him (page 58); Hesiod says that Zeus allowed his younger son to live for three generations.

The Cretan connection in this instance was founded upon place-names. The youth Miletos was the eponym of the Cretan city of Milatos, and Sarpedon may have been a local name in Crete as well as in Lycia. When mythographers found names of places or people even remotely resembling each other, they assumed personal relationships between them. The real connection of identical names was of course linguistic, the pre-Hellenic languages of Greece being closely related to some of the Anatolian dialects. But the habit of personification, prominent in all Greek thought, was inseparable from the ethnographical process, where it had a specious appearance of reality. River-gods and mountain-nymphs already existed in religious cults; in addition to these and largely combined with them in artificial genealogies, every nation, tribe, country, province and city had its eponymous founder, whose previous existence and subsequent adventures were adapted to racial or territorial theories. Lycia, which had been furnished with a royal dynasty from two Greek sources, Corinthian and Cretan, is said by Herodotus to have acquired its name from an Athenian Lycos, who had quarrelled, like Sarpedon, with his brother, the father of Theseus.

The persons thus created might legitimately stand as symbols in an ethnographical scheme, but they were accepted and perhaps proposed as real. It may seem strange to find a critical historian so intelligent as Herodotus or so intolerant as Thucydides repeating these fables as if they were matters of fact; but they were the basic materials of Greek education. Herodotus represents Xerxes as attempting to detach the Argives from the Greek confederacy before his expedition in 480 B.C. on the ground that 'the Perses from whom we descend was the child of Perseus the son of Danaë and Andromeda the daughter of Cepheus', and the Persians were therefore overseas kinsmen of the Argives. He explains in detail how this happened:

It was not until Perseus the son of Zeus and Danaë visited Cepheus the son of Belos, and marrying his daughter Andromeda had by her a son called Perses (whom he left behind him in the country because Cepheus had no male offspring) that the nation took from this Perses the name of Persians.

Similarly the Medes were 'anciently called by all people Arians, but when Medeia the Colchian came to them from Athens they changed their name'.

There is a notable example of etymological history in Thucydides' account of the Amphilochians. At the time of the Peloponnesian War they were a semi-barbarous tribe on the north-west border of the Greek mainland, between Acarnania and Epeiros. The name of their principal town was Argos, and it had therefore to be related to Peloponnesian Argos of the heroic legends. Thucydides says:

Amphilochian Argos and the rest of Amphilochia was founded by Amphilochos son of Amphiaraos when he returned from the Trojan War and was dissatisfied with the state of affairs at Argos. He named the town Argos after his own city; it was the largest town in Amphilochia and had the most considerable inhabitants. But many generations later they were compelled by misfortune to share the place with the neighbouring Ambraciots, and acquired from them the Greek language which they speak now, but the other Amphilochians are barbarians:

that is to say, their language was not Greek. If the people were barbarians, Amphilochia must have been the Greek version of a foreign name.

The Greeks could not transliterate alien words but reproduced them in Greek forms without much consideration of phonetics. Dareios, Xerxes and Artaxerxes are very distant echoes of the Persian Daryavaush, Khshayarsha and Artakhshatra; and it is worth noting that the Persian name of Artaxerxes is not related to that of Xerxes as Herodotus says it was, nor in any other way. Names were regarded as identical if they resembled each other at all in sound: thus the Egyptian Tirhaka appears in Greek as Etearchos. Amphilochos was a hero of the Returns from Troy, but had no place in the Homeric story, and the double coincidence in the names of the people and city of the Amphilochians reveals him as a mere eponym created to connect the lesser Argos with the greater.

Bellerophon's Corinthian grandfather, Sisyphos, is described in the *Iliad* as Aiolides, 'son of Aiolos'; not the guardian of the winds who gave Odysseus his most dangerous charges tied up in a leather bag, but the eponym of the Aiolic colonies. The three groups of colonies on the Asiatic coast were distinguished by their dialects as Aiolic, Ionic and Dorian. No province or people in European Greece bore the Ionian or Aiolic name, and the latter at least was not satisfactorily explained in Asia. The Greek word means 'variegated'. Hellanicos, who was himself an Aiolian of Lesbos, explained its use in that connection by the theory that the original colonists were a mixed lot. But the names were the basis of an elaborate scheme which professed to record Hellenic origins.

Doros and Aiolos were sons of Hellen, who was the son of Deucalion, the sole survivor (with his wife Pyrrha) of the Greek deluge, which is dated by the Parian Chronicle to 1528 B.C. Aiolos was king in Thessaly, and had, according to Hesiod, five sons, 'Cretheus and Athamas and artful Sisyphos, lawless Salmoneus and arrogant Perieres'. These carried the precious gift of Hellenism to previously barbarian tribes of northern Greece and Peloponnese;

their cousin Ion performed the same service for Attica; but the functions of Achaios were never satisfactorily determined, because there were two widely separated provinces of Achaia in historical times, and it was impossible to place him permanently in both of them. The family of Doros stayed in northern parts until the time came for their entry into the Peloponnese two generations after the Trojan War. In course of time five sons and seven daughters were added to the progeny of Aiolos, as various communities of the mainland put forward claims to the national inheritance, and Hellen himself was given another son, Amphictyon, the representative of Delphi, and a daughter Protogeneia, whose son Aëthlios was the eponym of the Olympic Games.

This tribal or cultural mythology had no reality in itself, but heroes of the epic legends were affiliated to its fictitious characters, so that it is impossible to know where genealogical invention began and poetical tradition may have ended. Only two long pedigrees are set out in the *Iliad* besides that of the Lycian kings. Aineias tells Achilles all about the Trojan royal family, in which every person except perhaps himself and Priam is manifestly mythical. Diomedes of Argos asserts his claim to consideration by reciting his descent from Portheus of Aitolia through Oineus and Tydeus. Oineus, he said, stayed in Aitolia, but Tydeus sought fortune and a king's daughter at Argos. Diomedes was a hero of the Trojan War, Tydeus of the Theban War, but Oineus was the eponym of an Aitolian tribe, the Oiniadai, and Portheus (whatever his name may have meant) was not a personage of heroic legend. He was afterwards affiliated to Pleuron of Aitolia, whose name is that of a place in the Homeric *Catalogue*.

Homer was not much interested in genealogies, though he makes Nestor say that old Peleus wanted to know 'the lineage and parentage of all the Greeks' who were at Troy. A man's grandfather is mentioned in the *Iliad* if there is anything to be said about him; if he was particularly distinguished his name might be used instead of the father's as the grandson's patronymic. Thus Achilles is either Peleiades (son of Peleus) or Aiacides (grandson of Aiacos).

7 Dancing-girl on a dinner table. Bronze statuette from Chiusi, form-
ing the base of a lampstand (Graeco-Etruscan, about 460 B.C.).

8 Inscribed clay tablets, and a magazine of the Palace, at Cnossos.

These patronymics were surnames, distinguishing one person from another, and could be used without the personal names. They marked the bearer's family but not his degree of descent. The three long pedigrees of Aineias, Diomedes and Glaucos would be in any case exceptional, but the introduction of fictitious personages from ethnographical and religious myth is more appropriate to the artificial schemes of Hesiod than to the heroic legends of Homer. Either these passages are later interpolations or the construction of symbolic genealogies had begun before the time of Homer.

Two more Asiatic legends which were adopted into Greek history, those of Memnon and the Amazons, are barely mentioned by Homer and in passages which seem to have been interpolated. Memnon, whose fictitious march from Susa gave Eratosthenes the date that is now regarded as traditional for the Fall of Troy, does not appear in the *Iliad* but is commemorated in the *Odyssey* by the garrulous Nestor as the person who had killed his son Antilochos and as the handsomest man at Troy, presumably on the Trojan side. He was the son of the goddess Eôs (Dawn) and Tithonos, whom Aineias cites in his pedigree as a brother of Priam, and whom Homer knows elsewhere as the consort from whose bed Dawn rises at break of day: that is to say, he was a purely mythical personage.

Memnon's men, the Ethiopians, are not named in the *Odyssey* as combatants, but as a blameless people living at the ends of the earth beside the streams of Ocean, to whom the gods make long journeys from Olympos. They were natives of the bright land of the rising sun, the Greek word *aithiops* meaning radiant. Poseidon, in the *Odyssey*, was away on one of these visits when Athena took the opportunity of persuading Zeus to set Odysseus on his homeward way. Two lines in this episode, which look like a pedantic gloss, add a new fact about the Ethiopians:

> *Who live in two places, most distant of men,*
> *Some where Hyperion sets and some where he rises.*

The western Ethiopians were the Sudanese or Nubians of southern Egypt. Their intrusion into the legend reflects the growth of geographical knowledge and provides some chronological information. Herodotus distinguishes the two countries and their inhabitants in his description of the Persian army that invaded Greece in 480 B.C.

The eastern Ethiopians (for there are two nations of that name) were brigaded with the Indians. They differed from the other Ethiopians, who came from the region above Egypt, in nothing but their language and the nature of their hair, for the eastern Ethiopians have straight hair, whereas those of Libya are more woolly-haired than any other people in the world.

Libya meant the whole of Africa outside Egypt.

Dark-skinned Asiatics from the shores of the Indian Ocean could have become known to the Greeks soon after the establishment of the Ionian colonies. But Greek penetration of Egypt, which brought the knowledge of negroid tribes beyond the cataracts of the Nile, did not begin before the seventh century, when native rulers with Ionian assistance threw off Assyrian control. Black men were doubtless seen in Syrian ports and on Phoenician ships before contact was resumed with Egypt, for the last dynasty before the Assyrian conquest was Nubian; but Greeks could not have known precisely where they came from. Hesiod places them vaguely in the south, where they were burned black by the winter sun withdrawn from Greece. When the country of the Nubians was located in Upper Egypt, its inhabitants were naturally identified with dark-skinned Indians, and shared with them the legend of Memnon as well as the Ethiopian name.

Memnon is a name of the common type in which an apparently Greek form covers an unknown foreign word. Its origins seem to have been Asiatic, perhaps Anatolian. Herodotus and others call Susa the city of Memnon, and say that he built the Persian palace there which was called the Memnoneion; but they do not say that this was its native name. Pausanias says that the Phrygians showed

the road by which Memnon marched his Ethiopians to Troy, and
Diodorus says that it was called Memnonian. It was doubtless the
Persian royal road from Susa to Sardis which Herodotus describes
in detail. He says that on its extensions from Sardis to Smyrna and
from Ephesos to Phocaia there were two rock-cut figures of a man
eight feet high holding bow and spear, which he identified with
the fabulous Sesostris:

His costume is half Ethiopian, half Egyptian. There is an inscription across the breast from shoulder to shoulder in the sacred
letters of Egypt, which says 'With my own shoulders I conquered
this land'. The conqueror does not say who he was nor where he
comes from, though elsewhere Sesostris records these facts. Hence
it has been imagined by some of those who have seen these figures
that they are Memnon's, but such as think so are far from the
truth.

Herodotus was connecting these reliefs with the rock-cut bound-
ary records of Rameses II and Esarhaddon near Beirut. His interpretations are obviously wrong, but the descriptions are remark-
ably accurate.

His figure on the rock near Smyrna is still visible. It stands about
a hundred feet above the river in the gorge of the Kara Bel, and
represents a war-god armed in Hittite fashion and wearing a
peaked helmet and shoes with turned-up toes. The inscription, in
Hittite hieroglyphs, is in the space between the head of the figure
and the spear. It could not have been identified in Greek times,
and is too badly weathered to be read now, even if the script were
known. This is the most westerly monument of the Hittite Empire, and belongs to the fourteenth or thirteenth century B.C.
(Plate 4).

Memnonian monuments were more numerous and imposing in
Egypt. Diodorus says that the Nubians denied Memnon's Asiatic
origin, and showed an ancient palace of their own which they
called by his name. There were other palaces and tombs of Memnon at Egyptian Thebes and Abydos, belonging to Pharaohs of the
Eighteenth Dynasty. The most notorious piece of misappropri-

ated property was one of the two colossal statues of Amenhotep III at Thebes, which are nearly sixty feet high. Greek historians attached this to Memnon because they looked for him in Egypt, the statues were conspicuous, and any name compounded with Amen or Amon was near enough to Memnon for their purposes. They identified him with the northern colossus, which was broken in two in early times, for a particular reason. Pausanias tells the story best:

The colossus in Egypt made me marvel more than anything. In Egyptian Thebes, on crossing the river to the tunnels [tombs of the kings] I saw a seated statue which has a voice. It is generally called Memnon, for they say that he came from Ethiopia [Nubia] to Egypt and advanced as far as Susa. The Thebans say the statue is not Memnon's but that of an Egyptian named Phamenopha, and I have heard some say that it is Sesostris. Cambyses broke it, and now it is thrown down from the head to the middle, but the rest is seated, and every day as the sun rises it cries out. One could best liken the sound to a lyre with a broken string.

The cry was of course Memnon's daily greeting to his mother. The vocal phenomenon is attested by earlier and later writers. Strabo was interested enough to be on the spot at daybreak, and heard a noise like a slight knock:

I was there with Aelius Gallus and his company of friends and soldiers, and heard the noise about sunrise, but whether it came from the base or from the statue or was made on purpose by one of the people who were crowding round the base, I am not able to affirm. Without a reasonable explanation of the cause one would believe anything rather than that the sound was emitted by stones so fixed.

The voice was said to have been silenced when the statue was repaired by one of the Roman emperors, but Eusebius says that it persisted until the birth of Christ.

Tithonos, Memnon's father, not being a hero of the Trojan War, had no place in realistic Greek legend, and his end was as mythical as his beginning. Eôs obtained the gift of immortality for him, but omitted to ask Zeus for agelessness, so that Tithonos withered up but could not die. His story is told in the Homeric *Hymn to Aphrodite*:

When the first grey hairs began to flow from his lovely head and his noble chin, the Lady Dawn kept away from his bed. But she kept him in the house, tended him with ambrosial food and beautiful garments. When loathly age bore full upon him, and he could not move nor lift his limbs, this seemed to her the best thing to do: she put him in a room and shut the shining doors, where he babbles endlessly and has no strength.

Later stories said that he was turned into a grasshopper. But Tithonos is a more substantial figure than many characters of the heroic legends, since the resemblance of his name to that of the principal god of Nubia, Didun or Dedun, can hardly be accidental, and his adoption by Greek mythographers must be dated to their first contacts with Egypt, or later. Memnon had to have a father, and none could be more appropriate there than the Nubian god. Tithonos is for once an accurate Greek reproduction of the foreign name.

Egyptian control of Nubia began in the Twelfth Dynasty. Senusret III (Sesostris) marked his southern frontier with two fortresses, Semna and Kumma, on opposite sides of the Nile about thirty miles above the Second Cataract. That frontier seems to have been lost during the anarchy of the Semitic (Hyksos) occupation of Egypt, but was restored and passed by the Pharaohs of the Eighteenth Dynasty. At the beginning of the fifteenth century Thothmes III rebuilt the temple which Senusret had set up at Semna, dedicating it to Khnum, the Egyptian god of the cataracts, and Dedun or Didun, the god of Nubia. Dedun is regularly commemorated in the new inscriptions on the temple walls, and is represented as embracing Thothmes at a shrine of Senusret (page 102). The dedicatory inscription reads (in Breasted's translation):

The good god Menkhepere (Thothmes III). He made (the temple)

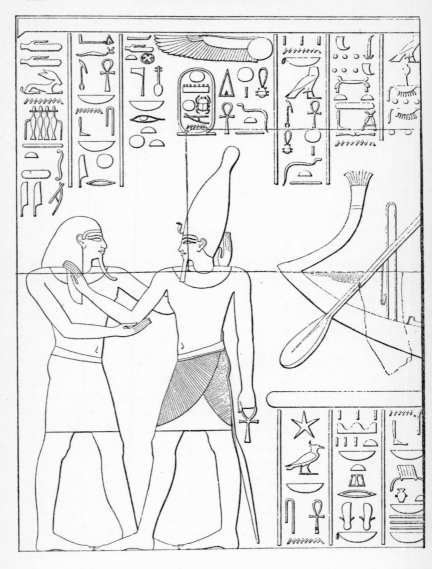

Thothmes III embraced by the god Didun.

as a monument for his father Dedun, Presider over Nubia, and for the king of Upper and Lower Egypt, Khekure (Senusret III).

The Twenty-fifth Egyptian Dynasty was Ethiopian in the sense that its Pharaohs were originally viceroys at Napata in the far south, and the troops with which they imposed their rule were at least negroid. The last effective king of the dynasty, Tirhaka, was driven from Lower Egypt by the invasion of Esarhaddon in 671 B.C. An Assyrian boundary-relief, at Zenjirli in North Syria, shows Tirhaka as a negro kissing the hem of Esarhaddon's garment.

Egypt was held by the Assyrians until Psamatik, first Pharaoh of the Twenty-sixth Dynasty, secured his independence with the support of Ionian and Carian mercenaries about 650 B.C. That was the occasion of the reopening of Egypt to Greek commerce and travel. Psamatik established his Greek troops permanently in garrison-towns and his successors opened the country to Ionian merchants through trading-posts on the Nile.

Herodotus, as a traveller in Egypt, was particularly interested in these developments:

The Ionians and Carians who had served with Psammetichos were given by him places to live in called the Camps. They were opposite each other across the stream of the Nile. The Ionians and Carians lived for a long time in these places, which are near the sea a little below the city of Boubastis, on the mouth of the Nile called Pelusian. King Amasis removed them long afterwards and stationed them at Memphis as his bodyguard against the Egyptians. We Greeks have been in touch with them since their establishment in Egypt, and therefore have precise knowledge of all Egyptian events in the time of Psammetichos and subsequently, for they were the first people of foreign speech to live in that country.

The earliest Greek historical inscription that we possess was cut on the leg of a statue of Rameses II at Abu Simbel, between the First and Second Cataracts, during a Nubian expedition of the second Psamatik about the year 596. It reads, in rather illiterate Greek:

When king Psamatichos came to Elephantinê those who sailed with Psammatichos son of Theocles wrote this. They came above Kerkis as far as the river let them go up. Potasimto led the foreigners, Amasis the Egyptians. Archon son of Amoibichos, Pelecos son of Oudamos wrote us. Elesibios of Teos. Telephos of Ialysos ... wrote me. Python son of Amoibichos. Pabis of Colophon with Psammatas. Hagesermos. Pasiphon. Crithis wrote ... when the king sent the army with Psamatichos for the first time.

Greek travellers may not have had to go as far as the cataracts to find Didun, but there is no record of his worship at Thebes or in Lower Egypt. The name of Dido (*Didon-*), Virgil's prehistoric queen of Carthage, is the same as his. Her name as the legendary founder of the city was Elissa, and Virgil does not say how she came to change it. Dido was in fact the goddess of Carthage, and as such was easily identified with the founder by Greek and Roman historians. The name has not been satisfactorily explained. Modern etymologists have looked for Semitic connections because the colony and the language were Phoenician, but the people were largely African, and an Ethiopian deity or title of a deity might exist as well in Libya as in Nubia. Dido appears to have been the Protector of Carthage as Didun was Protector of Nubia.

The two Homeric references to Amazons contain nearly all the historical information that we can expect about those people, whose Asiatic legend was certainly founded upon fact. In the *Iliad* they were one of the formidable powers against whom Bellerophon was despatched: that is to say, they were traditional enemies of western Anatolians. When Priam surveyed the Achaian forces from the walls of Troy, he said he had never seen such an array since he went to reinforce the Phrygians on the banks of the Sangarios, 'on the day when the Amazons came'. There they were raiders from the east. Homer's Amazons were women fighting on equal terms with men, but he says no more about them. The story of their change of front, as allies of Troy instead of enemies, appears first in the *Aithiopis*, the immediate sequel to the *Iliad*, but the only statement there which may have historical significance is that their queen Penthesileia was a Thracian: that is to say, the early Ionian geographers connected the Amazons with people living on the European side of the Black Sea. Hesiod placed them on the Asiatic side, in the country around the river Thermodon beyond the Halys, where their principal city was Themiscyra. That was their classical habitat.

In course of time, when these places became known but no Amazons were found in them, they were located farther east, in inaccessible regions of the Caucasos. There was always a belief in their existence, real enough in Strabo's time for him to examine critically:

There is a strange thing about the legend of the Amazons. Our accounts of other peoples make a distinction between mythical and historical elements, for statements that are ancient and mar-vellous and fictitious are called myths, but history seeks truth, whether old or new, and contains no marvellous element, or rarely. But the same stories are told now about the Amazons as in ancient times, although they are marvellous and incredible. For instance, who could believe that an army of women or a city or a tribe could ever be organised without men, and not only be organised but attack the territories of other people, and not only overpower the people near them to the extent of advancing to what is now Ionia, but even send an expedition across the sea as far as Attica? Even at the present time these tales are told about the Amazons. Themiscyra and the plains that lie around the Ther-modon and the mountains above them are mentioned by all writers as having belonged to the Amazons, but they say they were driven out of those regions. Only a few writers make asser-tions as to where they are now, but their assertions are unsup-ported by evidence and are beyond belief, as in the case of Thalestris, queen of the Amazons, with whom they say Alexander cohabited in Hyrcania in order to produce a child. This assertion is not generally accepted. Cleitarchos says that Thalestris set out from the Caspian Gates and the Thermodon to go to Alexander, but it is more than six thousand stades from the Caspian country to the Thermodon.

Cleitarchos was the historian who accompanied Alexander on his Asiatic expedition. Quintilian says of him that his ability was greater than his veracity.

At the beginning of his *Life of Theseus*, Plutarch makes a graceful apology for indulging in mythical history, but when he comes to the Amazonian attack on Athens, which is dated by the Parian Chronicler in the year 1256 (page 55), he writes as a serious historian:

That was evidently no mean nor feminine enterprise, for they would not have encamped in the city nor fought a hand-to-hand battle around the Pnyx and the Mouseion if their control of the country had not been so complete that they could approach the acropolis. ... To prove that the war ended with a treaty there is the place by the Theseion which is called Oathtaking (*Horcomosion*), and the sacrifice to the Amazons that was made before the Theseia. ... (Some of them were killed and buried in Megaris and Boiotia, where their tombs existed), and they did not even pass through Thessaly without coming into action, for their graves are still shown around Scotoussa and Cynoscephalai.

Herodotus did not doubt the reality of Amazons, but thought they were extinct, having crossed the Black Sea from the Thermodon to the Tanaïs (Don) and become progenitors of the Sarmatians. The Sarmatians of his day were a Scythian people living east of the Crimea; their women were still Amazonian, 'frequently hunting on horseback with their husbands, sometimes even unaccompanied; in war taking the field and wearing the same dress as the men'. He gives a romantic explanation of their voluntary loss of sexual independence.

In the middle of the thirteenth century several embassies or missions were sent to Mongol Courts in Asia by the Pope Innocent IV and the King of France. One of these envoys, the Franciscan Friar William of Rubrouck, stayed for some time with the Great Khan Mangu, grandson of Yenghiz Khan, at Karakorum in Mongolia, and addressed a report to Saint-Louis on his return. He says of the Mongol women (in Richard Hakluyt's translation):

All their women sit on horseback bestriding their horses like men. Moreover their women's garments differ not from their men's, saving that they are somewhat longer. When a great company of such gentlewomen ride together and are beheld afar off, they seem to be soldiers with helmets on their heads carrying their lances upright.

The customs described by Friar William and Herodotus may also be assumed for many tribes among the prehistoric nomads of the Russian steppes, and if some were Mongols, as is likely, the beardless faces of the men would give additional support to the idea of an army of women. The appearance and habits of the Amazons were manifestly borrowed from those of the Scythian horsemen in whom Herodotus thought they had been merged. Their military exploits in Anatolia were a traditional memory of the devastating raids from the other side of Caucasus which must have plagued that province in Hittite and Achaian times as they have done repeatedly since then.

The first Greek record of Scythian raiders is that of the Cimmerians in the middle of the seventh century B.C. They destroyed the kingdom of Phrygia, killed Gyges of Lydia in battle, and attacked several Ionian cities. Herodotus says that they entered Asia by the road along the east coast of the Black Sea, and were pursued by Scythians who lost them on the way and came in by the Caspian passes. It is unlikely that any of their victims could have known precisely where they came from, but they were evidently a number of hordes who raided east and west. Those in the east displaced the Median kingdom for a generation and became involved with the Assyrians; they contributed much towards the fall of Nineveh, ravaged Syria, and were stopped by Psamatik with arms or treasure on the borders of Egypt. These were the 'families of the north' of the Prophet Jeremiah, 'who shall lay hold on bow and spear, who are cruel and have no mercy, whose voice roareth like the sea, and who ride upon horses'.

Herodotus says that some of them plundered the temple of Aphrodite (Astarte) at Ascalon in Palestine and were consequently afflicted by the goddess with sexual impotence, from which their descendants in Scythia still suffered. This real or reputed element of effeminacy may also have contributed to the Amazon legend, of which the Cimmerian raids were a lively reminder. The stories of Ionian cities sacked or founded by Amazons must have come from those experiences. Finally the dress and weapons that the Greeks assigned to Amazons were the same as those of the Scythians in Xerxes' army, whom Herodotus describes as 'wearing trousers and having on their heads tall stiff caps rising to a point. They bore the bow of their country and the dagger; besides which they carried the *sagaris*'. That weapon, whatever its name may have meant, was always represented as a battle-axe.

Plutarch does not say that the graves of Amazons in Thessaly received heroic honours, but the hostility of their reputed occupants in life need not have precluded their worship after death. The only recorded cult of Amazons in European Greece was at Athens, where sacrifice was made to them on the day before the festival of Theseus. They were attracted to Athens by the artificial association of Theseus with Heracles, whose exploits were necessarily extended over the whole Greek world.

Heroes in the religious sense were local demigods tied in theory to the soil in which their bones were buried; but there were more heroes than bones, for some (as Hyacinthos at Amyclai) were pre-Hellenic gods, others (as Messene in Messenia) were political fictions. At the other end of the series were historical persons who were entombed and worshipped immediately after death. These were principally founders of colonial cities, as the great Miltiades in the Thracian Chersonese, of whom Herodotus says, 'After he was dead the Chersonnesians used to sacrifice to him, as is customary with an *oikistes*.'

Between these extremes was a multitude of epic heroes, many of whom had several tombs or cults which served as proofs of their legendary activities. Odysseus, for instance, was worshipped in Laconia, Aitolia, North Africa and South Italy, all those places claiming connection with his epic wanderings. But a sedentary hero could be transported from his native land, as Hector from Troy to Thebes. Pausanias says that the Boiotians imported his bones in obedience to an oracle; but his cult and tomb continued to exist in the Troad.

It was also possible to expel a hero if his presence became disagreeable. That was done in the late fifth century at Amphipolis in Thrace, where the Spartan Brasidas, who had been killed after liberating the city, was installed as hero in place of the Athenian *oikistes*. The most notorious instances of artifice in hero cult are those of Melanippos at Sicyon, Orestes at Sparta, and Theseus at Athens. Adrastos, leader of the two Argive expeditions against Thebes, had a tomb and a cult at Sicyon. Cleisthenes, tyrant of Sicyon in the sixth century, suppressed the recitation of Homeric poetry because it had so much to say about the glory of Argos, and proceeded to drive out Adrastos by interring his legendary enemy, Melanippos, by his side. He got the bones of Melanippos from Thebes. The story is told by Herodotus, who also relates in detail the Spartan discovery and appropriation of Orestes' bones from a previously unknown grave at Tegea. Plutarch records the pompous removal by Cimon, in 467 B.C., of the bones of Theseus from the island of Scyros to Athens. In both these instances the heroic skeletons were authenticated by their superhuman size. It is certain that the tomb or cult of a hero cannot be used as evidence for his place of origin or his human existence.

6

CYCLIC CHARACTERS

*Non-Homeric characters – Neoptolemos – Molossis and Dodona – Pyrrhos –
Epeirote and Macedonian genealogies – Athenian heroic pedigrees – post-
Homeric epics – Hesiod – the 'Catalogues of Women' – Cyclic poets – the
Trojan Cycle – Cyclic innovations – Thersites – Palamedes – Iphigeneia – the
Pelopid family.*

It was not only on the Asiatic side, where there was a void to be
filled, that alien or fictitious personages were introduced into the
tale of Troy. Some of the Greek heroes celebrated in Cyclic enlargements of the legend were local eponyms, as Palamedes and
his father Nauplios (the harbour of Nauplia and its rock-fortress
Palamídi); or characters from other legends, as Aithra the mother
of Theseus and her grandsons Demophon and Acamas; or sheer
inventions, as Achilles' son Neoptolemos. None of these are
Homeric in the sense that they take part in the action of the *Iliad*
or *Odyssey*, but Aithra and Neoptolemos have been awkwardly
interpolated in the texts in order to create authority for the Cyclic
innovations.

It cannot of course be assumed that people not mentioned by
Homer did not exist in the original legend, nor indeed that the
process of invention was not Homeric. Many of Homer's minor
characters have obviously fictitious names, as Thersites (Thruster),
who represents the democratic agitator. If we knew more names
of prehistoric places, tribes and deities, we could doubtless derive
many epic personages from them. But characters may be fairly
condemned as intrusive in the *Iliad* and *Odyssey* if their intrusion
can be explained or if they contradict the Homeric story. The
appearance of Aithra in one scene of the *Iliad* as a Greek servant

of Helen at Troy is unlikely, to say the least, in view of her advanced age and original dignity. The line was marked as an interpolation by the Alexandrian editor Aristarchos. Aithra was put in to connect the *Iliad* with Athens through the Cyclic story of the sons of Theseus, who were not known to Homer. His Athenians were led by Menestheus, but even they seem to have had no place in the original legend.

A son of Achilles is twice mentioned in the *Iliad* and once named as Neoptolemos; but that line was also rejected by Aristarchos. It is an essential element in the character and tragedy of Achilles that he was young and fated to die young: his old companion Phoinix reminds him that when Peleus sent him to Agamemnon he was only a boy. Achilles says himself that he has no wife, does not want one of Agamemnon's daughters, but will marry one of his own countrywomen if he ever gets home. Yet the *Odyssey* (perhaps interpolated from the Cyclic story) gives him a son old enough at his father's death to finish off the war. The name of Neoptolemos (New War) was appropriate to his function, and the simple Greek faith in names would find in it a proof of his reality.

The Cyclic stories and the interpolated passage in the *Iliad* put the birth and upbringing of Neoptolemos in the island of Scyros. The *Cypria* made him the grandson of its king Lycomedes, who had called him Pyrrhos (Red-head) in his childhood. There were various stories of Achilles' relations with Scyros. The *Cypria* said he was driven there by a storm and married the king's daughter. That was after the false start of the war (about which Homer knew nothing), when the Achaians failed to find Troy and put off the enterprise for nine or ten years. That interval and the nine years siege gave Neoptolemos time to grow up. The story of Achilles' concealment as a child among the daughters of Lycomedes, by a device of Thetis to save him from his fated death in battle, has the sentimentality of a Hellenistic invention. The only other allusion to Scyros in the *Iliad* gives a different and more realistic view of Achaian activities. The girl who slept with Patroclos, well-girdled

Iphis, was given to him by Achilles when he took steep Scyros, the city of Enyeus.

Neoptolemos was fetched from Scyros by Odysseus in the Cyclic story and became the mainstay of the Achaian attack. He had the honours of butchering Priam and Hector's child Astyanax, and of receiving Hector's widow Andromachê as the first prize of war. His brutal exploits were related in the *Little Iliad* and the *Sack of Troy*. In the *Returns* he was made to go overland to Epeiros, not to Thessaly or the northern Achaia where Achilles came from. Andromachê and he produced three sons in Epeiros, one of whom, Molossos, was the eponym of the Molossian people, and another the progenitor of the Epeirote kings. The later adventures of Neoptolemos were many and various, and supplied material for numerous Attic tragedies. He was ultimately buried in the precinct of Apollo at Delphi and became the tutelary hero of the place.

The Molossians, like other Epeirotes, were primitive people whom the Greeks called barbarians because their dialect was unintelligible. They had no independent place in history until the conquest of Greece by the Macedonians, to whom they were related. Alexander's fiery mother, Olympias, was a Molossian princess. Before that time their kings had native names reproduced in Greek as Tharrhypas, Arybbas, and the like; but after the entry of their Macedonian relatives and rivals into Hellenic society, they took the names of their Achaian ancestor, Aiacides, Neoptolemos or Pyrrhos. Pausanias says that King Pyrrhos of Epeiros, invader of Italy and nearly conqueror of Greece, who was killed at Argos in 272 B.C., was nineteenth in descent from the son of Achilles.

The reason for connecting Molossians with Neoptolemos is doubtless to be found in the famous prayer of Achilles in the *Iliad*: 'Lord Zeus of Dodona, dwelling far away and ruling at wintry Dodona, who didst ever hear my prayer and honour me.' Dodona was therefore the ancestral home of Achilles and in historical times was in the Molossian country. Pyrrhos, the second name of Neoptolemos, may have expressed the fact or fancy that red-haired individuals were not uncommon in Molossis, or he may have been the eponym of a Molossian tribe. That is the stuff of which ethnographical myth was made. It is significant that Pyrrha was the name given to Deucalion's wife, and that Dodona was said to have been founded by that primeval pair. There was a persistent idea that some northern tribes had red hair. Herodotus attributes it to the Boudinoi of Scythia, and Tacitus says the same thing about the inhabitants of Scotland.

Alexander the Great derived his descent from Achilles, which he celebrated at the tomb of his ancestor at Troy, from his Molossian mother. He was said to have taken Achaian armour from the temple there and to have left his own in exchange. Many Greek families, particularly at Athens, claimed and perhaps believed that they were directly descended from heroes of the epic legends, but their claims were no better founded than those ot Alexander and Pyrrhos and the Spartan kings. Apart from historical considerations, the violent break between Achaian and Hellenic cultures, no genealogical records could be accurately kept before the use of writing. The failure, for instance, of the Argive kings to preserve their short Dorian pedigree, so that even the lineage of Pheidon was unknown, reveals the general ignorance in these matters. But imagination was an active substitute for knowledge.

There are several indications of the time at which royal barbarians and noble Greeks began to establish their heroic ancestries. Plutarch says that Tharrhypas was the first Molossian king to adopt Hellenic manners and letters and to introduce humane laws into his kingdom, and also that he was fifteenth in descent from Neoptolemos. This seems to mean that the Achaian pedigree began with him. He was the great-great-grandfather of King Pyrrhos, and must have reigned about the middle of the fifth century. His neighbour in Macedon was the first king Alexander, who was also the first Macedonian Hellenist. Herodotus says of him:

Alexander son of Amyntas was an official representative and benefactor of the Athenians. The men of that family were acknowledged as Greeks by the administrators of the Olympic Games. When Alexander wished to compete at the Games and presented himself for that purpose, the Greeks who were to run against him objected on the ground that the contest was not for foreign competitors but for Greeks. But when Alexander showed that he was an Argive, he was received as Greek, and tied for the first place in the *stadion*.

The spectacle of a half-Oriental prince sprinting nude with democratic competitors is not convincing. He ought, like Pheidon and other famous people, to have won the four-horse chariot-race, of which there was no permanent record.

A hundred years later, when Macedon had become too formidable to be patronised by Athens, Demosthenes used very different language about King Philip:

He is not only not a Greek but is not connected in any way with Greeks, and is not even a foreigner from any reputable country, but a pestilent Macedonian, from a place whence one used not to be able to buy a decent slave.

'Used not', because Macedonian slaves were no longer available.

Herodotus recited the Macedonian pedigree as it was known to him: Perdiccas – Argaios – Philippos – Aeropos – Alcetes – Amyntas – Alexander. The alleged Argive connection began with Perdiccas:

who obtained the royal power in Macedon as I shall show. Three brothers of the lineage of Temenos, Gouanes, Aeropos and Perdiccas were banished from Argos to Illyria; they crossed into Macedonia and took service as bondsmen with the king for an agreed wage.

The story goes on as a fairy-tale, with the deception of the brothers by the wicked king and their magical deliverance by the youngest, who received with open arms the sunbeam offered to them by the king. A later enlargement of the pedigree is more plausible as a narrative but no more credible as history. Perdiccas is there fourth in descent from Caranos, a reputed brother of Pheidon of Argos, of whom Georgius Syncellus reports:

He raised a force from his brother (Pheidon) and the whole of Peloponnese, with which he made an expedition against the regions above Macedonia and took half the country.

Every important Athenian family or clan had an eponymous ancestor affiliated to an epic hero, and their pedigrees appear to have been constructed about the same time as those of the Epeirote and Macedonian kings. The Paionidai and Alcmaionidai chose descent from the Pylian Nestor through Paion and Alcmaion, his alleged grandson and great-grandson. The tyrant Peisistratos was in some degree a Neleid, and therefore (according to Herodotus) 'his father Hippocrates had the idea of naming him to commemorate the Peisistratos who was a son of Nestor'. The idea was evidently a new one at that time, the beginning of the sixth century.

Only one of these pedigrees has been preserved with any completeness, that of the Philaïd clan to which Miltiades and Thucydides belonged. Philaios was said to be a son of the Salaminian Aias, or a grandson, in which case his father was Eurysaces, whose name (Broad Shield) was a symbolical reminiscence of the Homeric shield of Aias, 'like the tower of a city wall'. The name of the clan was doubtless real, and the nominal relation of its eponym, Philaios, to Aias, would have been enough to initiate the Salaminian pedigree. That is fairly well recorded in the *Life of Thucydides* by Marcellinus: (Aias – Eurysaces –) Philaios – Daiclos – Epilycos – Acestor – Agenor – Olios – Lyces – Tophon – Laios – Agamestor – Tisandros – Hippocleides – (Cypselos –) Miltiades. This Miltiades was the founder of the Thracian Chersonese. The first historical person is Tisandros, but he is only known as the father of the famous Hippocleides, who lost his bride by standing on his head upon the dinner-table, a performance for which Greek dress was not designed.

Marcellinus cites Pherecydes and Hellanicos as authorities for the pedigree, but they may have repeated it from one of their immediate predecessors, Acousilaos or Hecataios. Herodotus says that Hecataios recited (and doubtless composed) his own divine pedigree (page 32). All these genealogies seem to have been fashionable by-products of sixth- and fifth-century mythography.

The tale of Hippocleides' dance told by Herodotus provides historical analogies for some elements and tendencies in prehistoric legend:

Cleisthenes, Tyrant of Sicyon, had a daughter whom he wished to marry to the best husband he could find in the whole of Greece. Having won the chariot-race at Olympia he made proclamation to the effect that whoever of the Greeks thinks himself worthy to be the son-in-law of Cleisthenes, let him come to Sicyon sixty days hence or sooner, for in a year's time, counting from the end of the sixty days, Cleisthenes will decide upon the marriage. So all the Greeks who were proud of themselves or of their country flocked to Sicyon as suitors, and Cleisthenes had a running-track and a wrestling-ground prepared to try their powers.

[Herodotus here names thirteen candidates who came from places as far apart as Molossis and Athens, South Italy and Thessaly.]

Cleisthenes examined them for a year, but the hardest trial of all was in the dining-room. When the day for the celebration approached, he made a great sacrifice of oxen and gave a great banquet. When dinner was over the suitors turned to music and general conversation. Presently, as the drinking progressed, Hippocleides, who quite amazed the others, asked the flute-player to play a dance; which he did, and Hippocleides danced to it. He fancied he was dancing extremely well, but Cleisthenes, who was watching him, began to mistrust the whole business. After an interval Hippocleides called for a table, and when it was brought he got up on it and danced first some Laconian figures and then some Attic ones; after which he stood his head on the table and began to wave his legs about.

Though Cleisthenes now hated the idea of Hippocleides as a son-in-law, still, as he wished to avoid an outbreak he restrained himself during the first and second dance; but when he saw him waving his legs in the air he could no longer contain himself, but called out, 'Son of Teisandros, you have danced your wedding away.' To which the other replied, 'Hippocleides doesn't care.' That was how the saying arose.

The tale was of course attached to Hippocleides to explain a saying which was current at Athens in the fifth century. He evidently had the reputation of the reckless aristocrat, like Alcibiades, but was sedate enough in later life to be eponymous archon in the year 566, in which the institution of the Panathenaic Festival was recorded. Nothing more is known about him.

The central theme of the wedding and the dance was a realistic Greek version of an animal fable, known in Indian folk-lore as The Dancing Peacock. The Golden Goose had a young daughter for whom he wanted to find a husband. So he summoned all the birds and bade her choose. She chose the peacock, who was so puffed up by his new importance that he spread his tail and danced, thereby exposing himself. The Golden Goose expressed strong disapproval, the little goose was shocked and refused to have the shameless fellow for a husband.

The attachment of a fable to well-known persons is characteristic of early Greek history and legend, as is also the accumulation of impressive names of participants in the event. Needless to say, the idea that a Greek princess could be thus offered in marriage is ridiculous, and precise record of thirteen persons present on any one occasion in the sixth century is impossible. Most of these young men are otherwise unknown and were probably fictitious; those that are known, Hippocleides and Megacles of Athens and Leocedes of Argos, the son of Pheidon, were not contemporary; and it is certain that no Molossian would have been admitted to Hellenic honours at that time.

The legendary model of the episode was the Wooing of Helen, in which all the Greek heroes of the Trojan War, and many others, competed; but Achilles, who would otherwise have been successful, was too young. A long list of them was recorded in the Hesiodic *Catalogues of Women*, and is partially preserved in some papyrus fragments. The only plausible element in the story of

Herodotus was the dance of Hippocleides, but that is demonstrably untrue of him on that occasion, which must have been about the time of his archonship.

It has however a factual interest, for dancing on the table was evidently a common after-dinner diversion, and one which demanded skill and care on the part of the performer. The point was that the Greek dinner-table had an oblong top but only three legs, one at each end of one short side and one in the middle of the other. If the dancer put a foot outside the triangle of the legs, the table would go over. Hippocleides would therefore not have been as drunk as Herodotus seems to imply. But his performance, without standing on his head, was not one for polite society, as is shown by a small bronze figure of a girl standing modestly on a dinner-table but wearing only her boots (Plate 7).

Literary exploitation of the oral epos, which began with Homer in the ninth century, progressed in two divergent directions, which may be called the romantic and the analytical. The Cyclic poets added persons and incidents, the school of Hesiod built up historical systems by means of genealogies. Both processes were necessarily inventive, and having no other instrument of expression than epic verse, both enjoyed the traditional authority of the Muses. The rivalry of the two schools explains the enigmatic statement of the Hesiodic Muse in the prelude to the *Theogony*: 'We know how to utter falsehoods that seem like truth' (historical romance) 'but we know how to tell the truth when we want to' (scientific analysis). The first line is cleverly lifted from the *Odyssey* and turned against the Homeric school. It is there applied appreciatively to a lying tale with which Odysseus deceives Penelope.

Hesiod was a name attached, like Homer's, to a large body of early poetry, epic in form but various in content. The three poems that are extant, *Works and Days*, *Theogony*, and *Shield of Heracles*, illustrate the methods of Hesiodic composition but give only a partial view of its material. The *Works and Days* is a philosophical and practical homily on good behaviour, duty towards the gods, duty towards one's neighbour, and duty towards oneself, ad-

dressed to an unsatisfactory brother, Perses. It is unique in supply-
ing biographical details about its author, the son of a returned
emigrant from Aiolis who established himself on a farm at Ascra
in Boiotia, but it does not give the poet's name. Hesiod is mentioned ambiguously in one of the two or three preludes to the
Theogony, where his inspiration is attributed to the Boiotian Muses
of Mount Helicon; but the local society which commemorated
him in the time of Pausanias claimed, with good reason, that only
the *Works and Days* was his. They showed a copy of it engraved
on lead.

The *Theogony* is a genealogical structure exhibiting the origins
and relationships of supernatural personages, from primeval
Chaos and the first parents of the gods, Earth and Sky, through
their Titanic progeny with its by-products of monstrosities and
abstractions, to the Olympian family peaceably domesticated after
battling with its turbulent seniors. The *Works and Days* provides
valuable information about social conditions of the age in which
the poet lived, but neither it nor the *Theogony* makes any definite
contribution to the history of Greece before Homer. The third
poem, the *Shield of Heracles*, is an excerpt from the *Catalogues of
Women*, the longest and most ambitious of the Hesiodic productions.

The *Theogony* ends with a list of goddesses who bore mortal
children, Eôs and Memnon, Thetis and Achilles, Aphrodite and
Aineias, and some others; and the poet invites the Muses to tell
next of 'the tribe of women': that is to say, the very much longer
tale of heroic children borne to gods by mortal mothers. The
Shield begins abruptly with the story of Alcmena, whose merits
attracted the attention of Zeus and were rewarded by the birth
of Heracles:

> Or she who left her home and native land
> And came with bold Amphitryon to Thebes,
> Alcmena, daughter of Electryon.
> She of the tribe of womankind was first

In beauty and in stature, and none else
Of mortal birth could vie with her in wisdom.

Each heroine was introduced in the *Catalogues* by the Greek words meaning 'Or she who – ', and the phrase was commonly used as an alternative title for the whole work, *Eoiai*. In this excerpt the poet explains how Amphitryon came to be away from home, how Zeus profited by his absence, and how Amphitryon came back. The rest and the greater part of the poem is taken up with descriptions of the battle of Heracles with Athena's aid against Ares and his son Cycnos, and of the shield made by Hephaistos for Heracles on the pattern of the shield of Achilles in the *Iliad*.

These romantic episodes in the genealogical *Catalogues* show that the products of the school of Hesiod were not very different from those of the followers of Homer. Many poems of the Epic Cycle were Hesiodic in the sense of being cosmological or ethnographical, and the Cycle was a representative series selected by Alexandrian or later scholars from the whole mass of early mythological epics. Titles of at least forty such poems are cited in ancient literature, but we do not know how many of them were put together in the Cycle. Proclos said they were not selected for poetical merit, but for the continuous narrative that they presented. Homer and Hesiod were ultimately distinguished as the first and greatest of the poets; the others, whether they were in the Cycle or not, were commonly and not always respectfully called cyclical. In its narrower and better sense that term was nearly equivalent to canonical.

A few traditional names, more likely to be real than Homer's, were available for distribution among these poets, but were not securely attached to particular poems. Thus Athenaeus, referring to the author of the Cyclic *Titanomachy*, calls him 'Eumelos of Corinth or Arctinos or whoever may rejoice in that appellation'; and again, 'The poet of the *Aigimios*, whether he was Hesiod or Cercops of Miletos'. But the poems were usually cited anonymously, as by Aristotle: 'Those who composed the *Heracleid* and the *Theseid* and things of that kind'. Pausanias applied a severely practical judgment to these literary problems:

The epics called Naupactian by the Greeks are generally ascribed to a Milesian author, but Charon (of Lampsacos) says they were by Carcinos of Naupactos. I am of the same opinion as the Lampsacene, for what sense would there be in giving the name Naupactian to poems about women by a Milesian?

From which we learn at least that the *Naupactia* were genealogical epics like the Hesiodic *Eoiai*.

These names, though placed conjecturally in time, seem to be historical because they were identified with places to which the persons belonged: Arctinos of Miletos, Cinaithon of Sparta, Eumelos of Corinth, Stasinos of Cyprus, Creophylos and Asios of Samos, Lesches of Mytilene, Agias of Troizen, Eugamon of Cyrene, and others. If Hesiod of Ascra be added, European Greece was as strongly represented among the Cyclic poets as the Asiatic homeland of the epic.

Arctinos, Cinaithon and Eumelos were placed by the literary chronographers about the First Olympiad (776 B.C.), Eugamon about the Fifty-third (568). Two hundred years seem to be too many for the production of the Cyclic epics, and the upper date, which was certainly conjectural, does not recognise the great gulf fixed between Homer and his imitators. It is safer to approach the chronology from the nearer end. Eugamon's date ought to be historical, for the North African colony of Cyrene was founded towards the end of the seventh century, and the reigns of its earliest kings were correlated with those of their Egyptian neighbours.

The Greeks called these traditional or anonymous poets the 'ancients' (*archaioi*); the 'moderns' (*neôteroi*) were the known authors of classical times. Eugamon, as the poet of the *Telegony*, was the last of the ancients; Panyassis, the Carian uncle of Herodotus, who wrote historical epics at the beginning of the fifth century, was among the first of the moderns. By that time the epic was nearly dead, and it remained so until it was revived by

Alexandrian scholars as an academic curiosity two or three hundred years afterwards. Panyassis indeed seems to have paid for his devotion to the past by losing credit for some of his own work. Clement of Alexandria says that he pirated his *Oichalia* from Creophylos of Samos.

It is probable that most of the Cyclic poets belonged to the seventh century; Hesiod may have lived at the end of the eighth. He says in the *Works and Days* that he won the prize for poetry at the funeral games of Amphidamas in Euboia. This Amphidamas must be the king of Chalcis who was killed in the Lelantine War with Eretria, of which Thucydides could only say that it was fought a very long time ago. Modern historians place it about the end of the eighth century. The reason for doubting the authenticity of this passage has been the desire to put Hesiod closer in time to Homer, but the strongly personal character of the *Works and Days* brings him nearer to the elegiac and iambic poets of the seventh century, Callinos, Archilochos and others, and the social and political developments reflected in his poem were moving towards democracy.

An astronomical statement in the *Works and Days* has been regarded as a possible source of chronological information:

> When sixty wintry days have run
> Since the turning of the sun,
> The star Arcturus rises bright
> From Ocean's stream at earliest night.

But it is computed that in the latitude of Helicon, sixty days after the winter solstice, Arcturus was not seen on the horizon at dusk before the fifth century; in the eighth century it was too high at nightfall to be described as rising from the sea. The Hesiodic error may have been in the determination of the solstice or in the interval between it and the twilight rising of the star; but the only reasonable inference from the statement is that the poet's astronomical and agricultural science was no more authentic than his history.

The *Theogony* and the fragments of the *Catalogues* bear no marks of individual authorship: indeed the *Theogony* has the appearance of being like the Athanasian Creed, the work of a long series of committees. When Pausanias had occasion to cite Hesiod, he was careful to add 'or one of his interpolators'. The Cyclic poems in their final forms were doubtless put together by individual poets, but their content must have represented the activities of some generations of collectors and inventors. The cosmological and genealogical epics contained the rudiments of theology and ethnology which were developed in due course by Ionian philosophers and geographers, but it cannot be said that the Cyclic elaborations of the Trojan legend made any acceptable contributions to history.

Materials available for these enlargements were remains of the oral epos, local cults of gods and heroes, ancient monuments and works of art, landmarks and natural phenomena, names of rivers, places and peoples, folk-lore and fairy-tales of Eastern Europe and Western Asia. It is unlikely that any historical traditions, beyond those that had originally been embodied in oral poetry, survived the disruptive and destructive effects of the last northern invasions. Even those comparatively recent events had left extremely vague and scanty memories because they had not been recorded in contemporarary verse. The foundation of the Asiatic colonies, the first definite event in Greek history, was less precisely documented than the Trojan War.

Survivals of the oral epos must have been fragmentary and local, but large enough to provide a basis for reconstruction of the principal legends. But the circumstantial narratives of theological and ethnological myth, which are necessarily fictitious, are evidence that the Greek imaginative genius could build imposingly without material foundations. It is possible indeed that Homer had used all existing fragments of the Trojan legend, and that the Cyclic poets completed the story by enlarging the adventures of his characters and introducing persons and episodes from other sources or of their own invention. These enlargements had their

origin in the natural desire to finish the tale told vividly but partially by Homer. A speaker in one of Plutarch's dialogues, discuss-
ing the pains and pleasures of historical research, says, 'We are
gripped by the story when we read the *Atlanticon* of Plato or the
last books of the *Iliad* and long for the rest of it, even if it is only
fiction.' That longing, in the case of the *Iliad*, was amply satisfied
by the Cyclic poets.

The oral epos, as represented in Homeric episodes, was not
popular poetry, but was produced by professional minstrels for
aristocratic audiences. The *Iliad* and *Odyssey* were designed for a
select class of listeners not less intelligent or fastidious than the
literary critics who ultimately separated these two poems from the
mass of inferior epics which had passed in the name of Homer for
three or four hundred years. The first use of writing would have
been followed by the practice of reading, not for general publication of the poems but for circulation among rhapsodes and their
schools. Publication was still oral and there was no prose literature.
The itinerant rhapsode became a popular performer, and his pro-
grammes were adapted to the intelligence of a new kind of listener,
whose applause was probably decisive in public competitions.

The blind poet of Chios appeals to the girls of Delos in his
hymn to Apollo: 'Who seems to you to be the sweetest of singers
that comes here, and in whom do you find most pleasure?'

We have so few fragments of the Cyclic poems that we cannot
judge their quality. The *Shield of Heracles* was recognised in antiquity as poor stuff, but some of the *Homeric Hymns*, which belong
to the same period, are good. Thucydides did not doubt that the
Hymn to the Delian Apollo was Homer's. Pausanias says that he
thought the *Thebaïs* was the best epic after the *Iliad* and *Odyssey*.
But Cyclic poetry as a whole, with its conventional phrases and
stilted diction, must have been tedious, and its principal means of
attraction was the narrative.

The contents of the Cyclic poems that completed the tale
of Troy are briefly recorded in the abridged summaries of
Proclos:

The poem called the *Cypria* is current in eleven books. Their contents are these. Zeus plans with Themis about the Trojan War. Strife appears while the gods are feasting at the marriage of Peleus and starts a dispute between Hera, Athena and Aphrodite about their beauty. Hermes leads them by command of Zeus to Alexandros in Ida for judgment; he favours Aphrodite, being bribed by marriage with Helen. At the prompting of Aphrodite he builds ships, and Helenos prophesies about what is going to happen to him. Aphrodite tells Aineias to sail with him. Cassandra reveals what will happen. Landing in Lacedaimon, Alexandros is entertained by the sons of Tyndareôs, and then in Sparta by Menelaos, and Alexandros gives Helen presents at a feast.

After that Menelaos sails for Crete, telling Helen to provide the strangers with what they need until they go away. Thereupon Aphrodite brings Helen and Alexandros together, and after that they load a great deal of property and put to sea by night. Hera raises a storm against them. Alexandros is driven to Sidon and captures the city. He sails away to Troy and celebrates his marriage with Helen. Meanwhile Castor was caught with Polydeuces stealing the cattle of Idas and Lynceus, Castor is killed by Idas, Lynceus and Idas by Polydeuces. Zeus grants them immortality on alternate days. After this Iris tells Menelaos what has happened at his house. He returns and plans the expedition to Troy with his brother, and goes on to Nestor. Nestor in a digression tells him the tale of the ruin of Epopeus after raping Lycos' daughter, the tales about Oidipous and the madness of Heracles, and about Theseus and Ariadne. Then they go through Hellas and collect the chieftains. They catch Odysseus, who pretends to be mad because he does not want to go on the expedition, by seizing his son Telemachos as a victim at the instance of Palamedes.

After that they assemble at Aulis and offer sacrifice. The incident of the snake and the sparrows is described, and Calchas foretells the future for them. Then they set sail and arrive at Teuthrania and sack the place as if it were Ilion. Telephos comes out in defence, kills Thersandros son of Polyneices, and is himself wounded by Achilles. As they sail away from Mysia a storm strikes them and they are scattered. Achilles puts in at Scyros and marries Deidameia daughter of Lycomedes. Then Achilles heals Telephos, who had gone to Argos in obedience to an oracle, so that he might be their guide for the voyage to Ilion.

When the fleet was assembled for the second time at Aulis, Agamemnon killed a stag in a hunt and said he was a better hunter than Artemis. The goddess was angry and kept them from sailing by sending storms. Calchas told them of the anger of the goddess, and instructed them to sacrifice Iphigeneia to Artemis, and they attempt to sacrifice her, having sent for her on the pretext of a marriage with Achilles. But Artemis snatches her away, takes her to the Taurians and makes her immortal. She puts a stag on the altar in place of the girl.

Then they sail to Tenedos. While they are having a feast, Philoctetes is bitten by a water-snake, and is left behind in Lemnos because of his nasty smell. Achilles quarrels with Agamemnon because he was invited to the feast too late. Then the Trojans oppose their landing at Ilion and Protesilaos is killed by Hector. Achilles drives them back, killing Cycnos son of Poseidon. They take up their dead and send envoys to the Trojans demanding the return of Helen and the property. When the Trojans refuse, they attack the city walls. Then they go out and devastate the country and the neighbouring cities. After that Achilles wants to see Helen and Aphrodite and Thetis bring them together.

Then the Achaians attempt to return home, but Achilles stops them. Then he drives off the cattle of Aineias, sacks Lyrnessos and Pedasos and several of the neighbouring cities, and kills Troïlos. Patroclos carries Lycaon to Lemnos and sells him, Achilles gets Briseïs as his prize from the spoils, and Agamemnon receives Chriseïs. Then comes the death of Palamedes, and the plan of Zeus to relieve the Trojans by withdrawing Achilles from the Greek forces, and a Catalogue of the Trojan allies.

Following this narration is the *Iliad* of Homer, after which come five books of the *Aithiopis* by Arctinos of Miletos with these contents:

The Amazon Penthesileia, a Thracian and daughter of Ares, appears as a Trojan ally. After distinguishing herself in battle she is killed by Achilles and the Trojans bury her. Then Achilles kills Thersites, who had slandered him and insulted him about his alleged love for Penthesileia. Dissension arises among the Achaians over the murder of Thersites. Consequently Achilles sails to Lesbos, sacrifices to Apollo, Artemis and Leto, and is purified from homicide by Odysseus.

Memnon son of Eôs comes to aid the Trojans, wearing armour made by Hephaistos, and Thetis tells her son the story of Memnon. In a battle Antilochos is killed by Memnon, then Achilles kills Memnon. Eôs begs from Zeus the gift of immortality for him. Achilles puts the Trojans to flight, and charging into the city with them is killed by Paris and Apollo. There is a great fight for his body, which Aias takes up and carries to the ships while Odysseus keeps back the Trojans. Then they bury Antilochos and lay out the body of Achilles. Thetis comes with the Muses and her sisters to lament her son, and after that she takes him from the funeral pyre and conveys him to the White Island. The Achaians build a mound for him and hold funeral games, and Odysseus and Aias quarrel over the armour of Achilles.

Next are four books of the *Little Iliad* by Leches of Mytilene, with these contents:

A trial is held for the armour and Odysseus wins it by contrivance of Athena. Aias in madness attacks the captured cattle of the Achaians, and kills himself. After that Odysseus catches Helenos, and he foretells how Troy can be taken. Diomedes brings Philoctetes from Lemnos. Philoctetes is cured by Machaon and kills Paris in single combat. Menelaos outrages the body, but the Trojans recover it for burial. After that Deiphobos marries Helen, Odysseus brings Neoptolemos from Scyros and gives him his father's armour, and the ghost of Achilles appears to him. Eurypylos the son of Telephos comes as a Trojan ally, is killed by Neoptolemos after distinguishing himself, and the Trojans are shut up in the city. Epeios builds the Wooden Horse to Athena's instructions, Odysseus disfigures himself and gets into Ilion as a spy. He is recognised by Helen and makes arrangements with her about the capture of the city. He goes back to the ships after killing some of the Trojans. After that he gets the Palladion out of Troy with the help of Diomedes. Then having put their best men into the wooden horse and burnt their huts, the rest of the Greeks set sail for Tenedos; but the Trojans, thinking themselves out of danger, take the wooden horse into the city, pulling down part of the wall, and rejoice as if they had defeated the Greeks.

This is followed by two books of the *Sack of Troy* by Arctinos of Miletos with these contents:

The Trojans are suspicious in the matter of the wooden horse, and stand around it considering what they ought to do. Some are for throwing it over the cliff, some for burning it. But others say they ought to make an offering of it to Athena, and their opinion is finally approved. So they turn to feasting and enjoyment as being free of the war. Meanwhile two snakes appear and kill Laocoön and one of his sons; the people of Aineias are alarmed by this portent and withdraw to Ida. Sinon having got into the city by false pretences, raises the fire-signal to the Achaians. They sail up from Tenedos, and the men from the wooden horse fall upon the enemy and capture the city with great slaughter. Neoptolemos slays Priam at the altar of Zeus Herceios where he had taken refuge. Menelaos seeks out Helen and takes her down to the ships after killing Deiphobos. Aias son of Ileus drags off Cassandra violently, and pulls the image of Athena away with her. The Greeks are incensed at this and want to stone him to death, but he takes refuge at the altar of Athena and escapes the danger that threatens him. Then the Greeks set fire to the city, and slaughter Polyxena at the grave of Achilles. Odysseus kills Astyanax, Neoptolemos takes Andromache as his prize, and they divide the rest of the booty. Demophon and Acamas find Aithra and take her away with them. Then the Greeks sail away and Athena devises destruction for them at sea.

The five books of *Returns* by Agias of Troizen join up with these. Their contents are as follows:

Athena sets Agamemnon and Menelaos at cross purposes about the embarcation. Agamemnon stays to propitiate the wrath of Athena, Diomedes and Nestor put to sea and get home safely. Menelaos sets sail after them and gets to Egypt with five ships, having lost the others at sea. The followers of Calchas and Leonteus and Polypoites make their way on foot to Colophon, where Teiresias dies and is buried. As Agamemnon's men are embarking, the ghost of Achilles appears and tries to stop them by foretelling what is going to happen. Then the storm at the Capherides rocks is described, and the destruction of the Locrian Aias. On instructions from Thetis, Neoptolemos makes his way by land, gets to Thrace and meets Odysseus at Maroneia and finishes his journey, burying Phoinix who dies on the road. He himself arrives in the Molossian country and makes himself known to Peleus. Then comes the vengeance of Orestes and Pylades on Aigisthos and Clytaimnestra for the murder of Agamemnon, and the home-coming of Menelaos.

The *Odyssey* of Homer comes after this, and then the *Telegony* in two books by Eugamon of Cyrene, with the following contents:

The suitors are buried by their relatives, Odysseus sacrifices to the Nymphs and sails to Elis to inspect his herds of cattle. He is entertained by Polyxenos and receives the gift of a wine-bowl. Then come the stories of Trophonios and Agamedes and Augeas. Odysseus sails back to Ithaca and performs the sacrifices prescribed by Teiresias. After that he goes to the Thesprotians and marries Callidicê, queen of Thesprotis. Then the Thresprotians led by Odysseus go to war with the Brygoi; Ares puts the forces of Odysseus to flight and has a battle with Athena, but Apollo stops them. Polypoites, son of Odysseus, inherits the kingdom after the death of Callidicê and Odysseus goes back to Ithaca. Meanwhile Telegonos, sailing in search of his father, lands on Ithaca and plunders the island. Odysseus comes out to defend it and is slain unwittingly by his son. When Telegonos finds out his mistake, he transports his father's body and Telemachos and Penelope to his mother. She makes them immortal; Telegonos marries Penelope, and Telemachos Circê.

The development of Cyclic episodes from brief or casual Homeric references is well illustrated by the opening of the *Cypria*, where the whole story of divine responsibility for the Trojan War was invented on the strength of two words in the fifth line of the *Iliad*, *Dios Boulê* (the Will of God). They are used there in a general sense: Homer calls upon the Muse to sing of the Wrath of Achilles which sent many valiant souls to Hades, 'and thus accomplished the Will of God'. The *Cypria* explained at length precisely what and why the Will of God was, and how it operated, from the initial conference of Zeus with Themis, goddess of Fate, through the Marriage of Peleus, the Judgment of Paris, and the Rape of Helen, to the misguided expedition that landed Achilles in Scyros and so created Neoptolemos, the final conqueror of Troy. The histories of people barely mentioned by Homer, Philoctetes and Protesilaos, Chryseïs and Briseïs, were told in full, and strange characters on both sides, Memnon and the Amazons, Telephos and Eurypylos, Demophon and Acamas, Palamedes, Iphigeneia and others, were added to the Trojan legend.

Homer's narrative is always convincing, and his demands upon religious credulity were not excessive. If the incidents and characters of the *Iliad* had not been so realistic, they would not now be so widely accepted as historical. Cyclic episodes are generally less plausible, and actions of the gods tend to become ridiculous. A scholiast commenting on the fifth line of the *Iliad* quotes the passage from the *Cypria* that gave the reason for the *Dios Boulê*:

There was a time when myriad tribes of mortals were a burden upon deep-bosomed Earth. Zeus saw, and determined in mercy and wisdom to relieve all-nurturing Earth of men by launching the mighty conflict of the Trojan War. So the heroes were slain at Troy, *and the Will of God was fulfilled*.

The last words were repeated from the *Iliad*.

The attribution of a sordid dispute to three great goddesses and its reference to a mortal arbitrator were contradictions of Olympian dignity and behaviour. Homer's deities were made after the image of his first audiences: their morals were loose but their intelligence and sense of propriety were acute. His gods made themselves known to individual mortals alone and usually in disguise; they did not appear in public or in companies as the *Cypria* made them do at Peleus' wedding and the *Aithiopis* at Achilles' funeral. These unorthodox epiphanies seem to be related to a demand for marvels and mysteries in real life which was not recognised in the *Iliad*.

Cassandra and Helenos foretell the disastrous future in the *Cypria* and *Little Iliad*; the ghost of Achilles appears three times on prophetic missions; Achilles heals the wound of Telephos miraculously; the lynx-eyed Lynceus sees his enemies across the Peloponnese and inside a hollow oak-tree; Achilles is transported by his mother from his funeral-pyre to the White Island in the Black Sea; Iphigeneia is turned into a hind on the altar of sacrifice, and her mortal body is translated to immortal life in the Crimea; Memnon and the brothers of Helen are made immortal by Zeus. The apotheosis of Odysseus' family in Circê's island was not even orthodox, for only Zeus could confer immortality, and he refrains from using that power in the *Iliad* and *Odyssey*.

Horror is added to mystery in the destruction of Laocoön and his son by two sea-serpents, and the human sacrifices of Iphigeneia and Polyxena are the first appearances of that bogey of Greek history. The murder of the child Astyanax by Neoptolemos or Odysseus was a classical example of brutality. It was described in terms that appealed to popular and artistic imagination, and so became a favourite subject in Attic vase-painting. Less brutal but more shocking to Greek sentiment was the violent mishandling of Cassandra by Aias, and the sacrilege thereby committed against Athena.

The Cyclic poets also introduced erotic motives, in which Homer had not been interested. The passionate love of Achilles for the dying Amazon was vulgar melodrama, but it is nobly illustrated by one of the greatest of the vase-painters, in contrast to the bestial perversions of the episode by later mythographers or parodists.

Religious and social developments reflected in these poems show that they were composed long after the *Iliad* and *Odyssey*. But many references to their continuations of the legend have been interpolated in Homeric texts, particularly in the *Odyssey*, where Nestor, Menelaos and Odysseus are made to recall incidents of the final scenes at Troy and describe the supreme absurdities of the Wooden Horse.

Literary, social and religious innovations are apparent in the Thersites episode of the *Aithiopis*. He is manifestly a fictitious character in the *Iliad*, set up as a figure of fun for the entertainment of aristocratic society. His name (Thruster) marks him as a type of the vulgar agitator, and Homer's description of his personal appearance, 'bandy-legged, lame of one foot, round-shouldered, narrow-chested, with a misshapen head and a scanty stubble on it', was a measure of the contempt in which such people were supposed to be held. When Odysseus thrashes him and threatens worse treatment, the army laughs, though some of them have just been subjected to the same kind of discipline. But his death at the hand of Achilles in the *Aithiopis* divides the army. Though Proclos did not say so in his summary, it was reported by later mythographers that Thersites was a cousin of Diomedes, and his noble birth was doubtless proclaimed in the *Aithiopis*. When Diomedes recited his own pedigree in the *Iliad* he mentioned an uncle, Agrios, whose name (Ruffian) gave the genealogists an obvious parent for the blustering Thersites. Thus Homer's dummy became a creature of flesh and blood, and the demagogue was promoted to a position of social importance.

Whatever might have been the consequences if Achilles had killed Thersites, or even Diomedes, in the *Iliad*, they would not have included ritual purification. Homeric homicides sought safely, when they were unable to defend themselves and their victims were persons of consideration, in a hasty change of domicile. They were received by powerful protectors, as Patroclos by Peleus, and that was the end of the matter. The complex religious procedure to which Achilles was subjected in the *Aithiopis* belonged to a later age. The trial by jury (for the armour of Achilles) was a democratic innovation. Knowledge of Ionian cities, which Homer had suppressed, appears in the name of Colophon, and the Crimea (Tauroi) and the White Island represent much later Milesian discoveries in the Black Sea.

Most of the new Cyclic characters, Telephos of Mysia and his son Eurypylos, Memnon and the Amazons, Cycnos and others, were Trojan allies who could not have belonged to an Achaian tale of Troy. The chief intruders on the Greek side were Iphigeneia, daughter of Agamemnon, who was a goddess; the sons of Theseus, Demophon and Acamas, who were imported from Attic legends; and Palamedes, a figure of Peloponnesian folk-lore.

Palamedes and his father Nauplios were local eponyms who took their names from the Argive port of Nauplia and the steep acropolis, still called Palamídi, which overlooks the harbour. Nauplios was a builder or wrecker of ships, as occasion required. His name has a plausible meaning (Navigator), but Palamedes must have been a pre-Hellenic word transposed into a familiar but irrelevant Greek form, as Sainte Marie-la-Bonne was reduced to 'Marrowbone' in English. The Greek words that came nearest to the sound were *palamê* (hand) and *mêdos* (craft), and Palamedes thus became the traditional handyman and inventive genius, a human Prometheus. He was said to have invented the alphabet, weights and measures, the athletic discus, dice, lighthouses and military tactics. His function in the enlarged Trojan legend was to compete with the wily Odysseus, but he did not last long there. There were several versions of his end: the *Cypria* said that he was drowned by Odysseus and Diomedes when they went out fishing, a most unlikely occupation for Achaian heroes unless they were driven to it on a desert island, as Menelaos said that he was.

One of the great wall-paintings by Polygnotos at Delphi represented the scene in Hades on the occasion of Odysseus' visit to the dead. Palamedes was shown there dicing with Thersites while the Locrian Aias watched their play. Aias still bore the marks of his watery end, according to Pausanias, who also says that these three were grouped together because they were on bad terms with Odysseus. The picture was nearly six hundred years old when Pausanias saw it.

It is seldom permissible to base positive statements upon the silences of Homer, but it is safe to say that he did not mention Iphigeneia because she was not known in his time as a daughter of Agamemnon. Tales of human sacrifice were doubtless current then as later, but Homer did not admit such crudities in his story. In any case, the sacrifice at Aulis, with its fatal consequences for the Pelopid family, had no relevance unless the victim was the king's daughter.

When Agamemnon was trying to appease the wrath of Achilles, he said he had three daughters of whom Achilles might choose any one for a wife, Chrysothemis, Laodicê and Iphianassa. This last name is often taken to be equivalent to Iphigeneia, but it is not, and one cannot juggle with the legends in that fashion. The story of the miraculous sacrifice and translation of Iphigeneia to Tauris was improved by Hesiod, who said that she was made a goddess, Hecate. Euripides tells the tale dramatically in his *Iphigeneia at Aulis* and its sequel *Iphigeneia in Tauris*. There, in the Crimea, she is the priestess of Artemis, charged with the duty of sacrificing strangers who arrive accidentally or otherwise by sea. Her brother Orestes is told by Apollo that as the final penance for killing his mother he must bring to Greece the image of Artemis from the temple. He comes with his friend Pylades, is duly arrested and prepared for sacrifice. There is a recognition scene and a fight, and Orestes and Pylades get away with Iphigeneia and the image. Euripides makes them land at Brauron, near Halai in Attica, where Athena had instructed them to institute a rite commemorating the deliverance of Orestes from sacrificial death. The speech of Athena is quoted from Gilbert Murray's translation of the play:

> Go on thy ways, Orestes, bearing home
> The image and thy sister. When ye come
> To god-built Athens, lo, a land there is
> Half hid on Attica's last boundaries,
> A little land, hard by Carystus' rock,
> But sacred. It is called by Attic folk
> Halae. Build there a temple and bestow
> Therein thine image, that the world may know
> The tale of Tauris, and of thee cast out
> From pole to pole of Greece, a blood-hound rout
> Of ill thoughts driving thee. So through the whole
> Of time to Artemis the Tauropole

Shall men make hymns at Halae. And withal
Give them this law. At each high festival
A sword, in record of thy death undone,
Shall touch a man's throat, and the red blood run,
One drop for old religion's sake. In this
Shall live the old red rite of Artemis.
And thou, Iphigeneia, by the stair
Of Brauron in the rocks the key shall bear
Of Artemis. There shalt thou live and die
And there have burial. And a gift shall lie
Above thy shrine, fair raiment undefiled
Left upon earth by mothers dead with child.

Euripides could not have recited this ritual to an Athenian audience if it was not so performed at Halai. Some other historical facts are supplied by Herodotus and Pausanias. Herodotus says in his survey of Scythian tribes that the Tauroi of the Crimea sacrificed to their Maiden Goddess (*Parthenos*) Greeks and other people who were driven to their shores by stress of weather, and that they said the goddess was Iphigeneia daughter of Agamemnon. He describes the mode of sacrifice in detail:

After the preliminary ceremonies they knock the victim on the head with a club. Then, according to some accounts, they throw the body from the cliff on which the temple stands, and nail the head to a cross. Others agree that the head is treated in that way, but say that the body is buried.

Scythians who were so inhospitable to foreign visitors could not have given their deity a Greek name nor connected her with the epic legend. The story of the sacrifices was doubtless exaggerated, but it records experiences of the first Greek venturers on the northern coasts of the Black Sea, where they found a native deity whom they identified with Artemis or Hecate, and a real or reputed practice of human sacrifice. Greeks regularly gave the names of their own gods and goddesses to foreign deities.

Iphigeneia was certainly a title of Artemis: the lexicographer

Hesychius states quite simply that she was Artemis. Among the notable monuments at Hermion in the Peloponnese Pausanias records a sanctuary of 'Artemis called Iphigeneia'; and again at Aigirai in Achaia: 'There is a temple of Artemis in which stands an ancient image: the inhabitants say it represents Iphigeneia daughter of Agamemnon.' The temple to which Euripides refers was at Halai, but he says that the women's clothes were dedicated to Iphigeneia at Brauron, where there was another famous cult of Artemis celebrated by the bear-dance of little Athenian girls. The old wooden image was at Halai but the original fetish was also shown at other places in Greece and Asia, notably at Sparta, where it was used in historical times to represent the formidable Artemis Orthia at the ritual scourgings of Spartan boys.

Many reasons can be found for the common religious practice of not calling deities by their proper names. The Greeks had more than most people, with their national habit of identifying pre-Hellenic and foreign divinities with members of the Olympian family. Every Greek god and goddess had numerous appellative titles expressing divine qualities or functions or local relationships: not less than sixty such epithets of Artemis are recorded, most of which were cult-titles. Iphigeneia was one of them. The name means 'mighty in birth', and expressed her power as a goddess of marriage and maternity. That is why the clothes were devoted to Iphigeneia and why the girls danced for Artemis at Brauron. The title of Artemis at Halai was Tauropolos, which meant originally 'Caring for Bulls', or something of that kind; but it was interpreted as 'Going to Tauris', and was evidently the starting-point of the whole story. Its invention must in any case be later in time than the first Greek contact with the Crimea, which can hardly be placed before the seventh century.

The name of Iphigeneia was equally appropriate to a princess of mighty birth, as indeed were those of Agamemnon's Homeric daughters, so much so that one may reasonably doubt their reality. Chrysothemis, Laodicê and Iphianassa celebrate the three prerogatives of Wealth, Jurisdiction and Dominion that belonged particularly to the lords of golden Mycenai and the sceptre of Pelops. Chrysothemis survived as an insignificant personage in Attic tragedy, but Laodicê and Iphianassa were displaced in the later legend by Iphigeneia and Electra.

The Pelopid family, which ought to have had the best-preserved pedigree, if there had been a real tradition in these matters, seems in fact to have had the worst, perhaps because professional genealogists gave most attention to it. Homer's account of the elder members is that Pelops gave his divine sceptre to Atreus, Atreus at his death left it to Thyestes, Thyestes left it to Agamemnon. This would naturally mean that the succession was from father to son, and at least implies that it was amicable. But in later or variant versions Atreus and Thyestes were brothers who quarrelled hideously, and the Homeric Atreidai, Agamemnon and Menelaos, were sons of one Pleisthenes, a brother or a son of Atreus, who died young. Two members of the family have tribal names which mark them as eponyms of the Thyestai and Orestai, barbarous people who lived in Illyria in historical times. Pelops is also a tribal name, but no such tribe was known; it may have been invented to explain the name of the Peloponnese, a process quite in accordance with the principles of ancient ethnography. Like Aiolos, the greater fictitious eponym of mainland Greece, Pelops was given large and increasing numbers of sons and daughters, whose function was to convey the honours of Achaian nobility to Dorian states.

7

CLASSICAL MYTHOGRAPHY

Epic authority – prose literature – logographers and genealogists – Hecataios – Acousilaos – literary fraud – Pherecydes – history and mythology – Hellanicos – lyric poetry – Stesichoros – Attic drama – Hellenistic poets – mythological handbooks – Apollodorus.

The old epic, works of Homer, Hesiod and the Cyclic poets, had biblical authority for the ordinary Greek citizen. These poets were the inspired prophets of the nation, and the subject-matter of the poems was at once religion and ancient history. References in later writers show that they covered the whole field of myth and legend, so fully that there can have been little for mythographers to do, after the middle of the sixth century, by way of addition to the narrative. Epic poetry itself seems to have come to an end at that point because its subjects were exhausted.

But the mass of material must have been hard to handle: numerous books existing in few copies, difficult of access, and as we know from the lamentations of Pausanias, who tried valiantly to use such of these primary authorities as existed in his time, full of contradictions. His efforts were worthy of a better cause, for his principle of seeking the original source was a sound one, but it often led to disappointment. 'As I very much wanted to know', he says in rehearsing the prehistory of Messenia, 'what children were born to Polycaon by Messenê, I read the *Eoiai* and the *Naupactia* and all the genealogies of Cinaithon and Asios as well. But there was nothing in them relevant to this question.' When he found agreement in some detail, he recorded it as if it were exceptional. Thus, 'the *Eoiai* and the *Minyad* agree about the manner of Meleager's death.'

The desirability of establishing consistent stories on that level doubtless led to the formation of the Epic Cycle, which led in its turn to the disappearance of the books that were not included in it. But long before that time the matter had been taken in hand by the mythographers who wrote in prose and became the secondary authorities.

The beginning of prose literature coincided in time with the first development of Ionian philosophy or science. The earliest philosophers might formulate their theories in verse, as Xenophanes of Colophon did, but that medium was ill adapted for criticism of rival theories, which is an essential element in intellectual progress. Prose writing therefore became the vehicle of imaginative and critical thought, and was applied about the same time and perhaps independently to historical research and record.

The first historical writings properly so called were annals compiled by attaching events to successive years of office of civic magistrates. Annals were in due course enlarged into chronicles, as in medieval Europe, and chronicles into more or less historical narratives. These enlarged Greek records (*Hôroi*) were extended upwards to the foundations of the cities (*Ctiseis*), and beyond them to the heroic adventures of their founders. History was thus half-smothered at its birth by myth and legend. Its deliverance was begun by the good intentions of Hecataios towards the end of the sixth century, and accomplished by the genius of Herodotus and Thucydides in the course of the fifth. But there were always Greek historians, as Hellanicos, Theopompos and Diodorus, who were mythically inclined, whether by their own beliefs or, as Thucydides affirmed, for popular appeal.

Cadmos of Miletos is the first historian whose name is recorded, but no word of his has survived, unless it be the title of one of his works: *The Founding of Miletos and All Ionia*. Since he was earlier than Hecataios, he probably wrote about the middle of the sixth century. The authors of these medleys of myth and history were called logographers (storytellers) by Herodotus and Thucydides; the term as used by the latter was certainly contemptuous. But

Hecataios, to whom Herodotus applied it, was a man of action and an observant traveller to whom Herodotus owed much of his geographical information.

If Hecataios had limited his activities to geographical observation and record, he would have had a higher place in scientific repute than the speculative philosophers who decried him. But geography involved him in ethnography, and ethnography in myth and legend, to which he tried to give reality by means of artificial genealogies. He defined his purpose in the first words of his *Histories*: 'This is the story told by Hecataios of Miletos. I write here what I consider to be true, for the tales of the Greeks are manifold, and in my judgment ridiculous.' Hecataios evidently did not have the respect for tradition that has been attributed to him by some modern writers. He, if anyone, was in a position to know that there were no oral traditions at that time, and he must also have believed that the tales of the epic poets which he criticised were as fictitious as his own corrections of them. He professed to reduce the current legends to reasonable terms in relation to his own knowledge and ideas. But he attempted to reform mythical history without rejecting it, and thereby incurred the ever-ready censure of his philosophical successor Heracleitos of Ephesos, who wrote, 'Much learning does not teach a man common sense, else it would have taught Hesiod and Xenophanes and also Pythagoras and Hecataios.'

The methods of Hecataios can be seen in some of his fragments that have survived. The Tenth Labour of Heracles was to bring to Eurystheus at Tiryns the cattle of Geryon, who was, according to Hesiod, a monstrous son of Chrysaor, brother of Pegasos, and lived in the island of Erytheia on the far side of Ocean. Erytheia was probably not precisely located in the original story, for Ocean was a stream which encircled the whole earth, but it is more likely to have been imagined in the east than in the west. When Geryon was brought into the Heracles legend and the Atlantic Ocean was discovered, it was placed off the coast of Spain beyond Cadiz. Heracles killed Geryon and his herdsman and his monstrous hound (brother of the Chimaira), and drove the cattle across Spain, over the Pyrenees and the Alps to Italy, and thence by devious routes, even through Sicily and Scythia, to Tiryns. Hecataios, as a geographer and a realist, could not accept these details of the story, but his improvement of them involved him in historical invention. Geryon, he said, had nothing to do with the Iberian country, nor was Heracles sent to an island Erytheia beyond the Great Sea (Mediterranean), but Geryon was king in Epeiros around Ambracia and the Amphilochians, and Heracles drove the cattle from that region of the Mainland. Aelian remarks in recording this transaction that even that drive was no mean feat. Needless to say there was no authority for placing Geryon in Epeiros, but Hecataios could not eliminate him altogether, and therefore put him at the greatest possible distance from the Argolid within the boundaries of Greece. His revised version was not generally accepted, for Herodotus in the next generation repeated the Spanish and Scythian adventures of Heracles as a tale told by the Greek colonists of the Black Sea. The home of Geryon in the original myth was certainly in Asia, where his father Chrysaor and his dog Orthos belonged.

Another correction of legend shows Hecataios moving ponderously in the right direction. He commented on the story of Danaos and his Egyptian brother and their trains of sons and daughters: 'Aigyptos did not go to Argos himself but his sons did; as Hesiod wrote, fifty; but as I say, not even twenty.'

Hecataios did at least attempt to relate the legends to reality, if not to truth, but other genealogists merely elaborated fictitious elements. One of the earliest of them was Acousilaos of Argos, who is described by Suidas as a very old historian, and associated with Cadmos by Josephus. He must have been a younger contemporary of Cadmos, who was generally celebrated as the first prose writer, and rather older than Hecataios, whose date is fixed by the fact recorded by Herodotus that he was involved in the revolt of the Ionian cities against Persia in 500 B.C. The literary activities of Acousilaos are probably well described by Clement of

Alexandria, who says that he turned the works of Hesiod into prose and published them as his own. That is to say, he produced a greatly needed prose version of the epic stories; but he selected or interpreted them to fit his own ideas.

The abandonment of metrical form necessarily involved a loss of authority for the content of literature, since prose writers could not claim the inspiration of the Muses. Suidas says that Acousilaos professed to have found his genealogical information on inscribed bronze tablets which his father dug up somewhere in his garden. The anecdote may well be true of Acousilaos, who certainly needed some immoral support in his bold venture, and who was born and bred in Boiotia, where epigraphic pretence and forgery were cultivated, as we have seen. In any case the story is interesting as the first appearance of that commonplace of literary fraud, the ancient document mysteriously acquired and accessible only to the author whose statements are based upon it. We shall meet it again with the self-styled Dares of Phrygia and Dictys of Crete.

An analogy in medieval England was the very ancient book in the British tongue brought from Brittany by Archdeacon Walter of Oxford and translated into Latin by Geoffrey of Monmouth as his *History of the Kings of the Britons*, from Brutus, great-grandson of Aineias and eponym of the British people, through King Lud, King Lear and King Cole, to the heroic Arthur. But the elementary deceit of Acousilaos turned to his disadvantage in a more sophisticated age, for Suidas reports elsewhere that his books were false.

The only known contribution of Acousilaos to the Trojan legend was a new interpretation of the Will of God that caused the war, in his case the will of Aphrodite. She knew an oracle to the effect that if Priam's house should come to an end, that of Anchises would rule at Troy, and therefore made love to him when he was old enough. Then she prepared the destruction of Priam and his sons by inspiring Paris with love for Helen, and took care throughout the war that the Trojans should not give Helen back. But the chief interest of Acousilaos seems to have been in genealogies, in which Josephus says that he corrected Hesiod and Hellanicos corrected him.

Acousilaos was superseded in the next generation by Pherecydes, probably because Pherecydes, who came from the island of Leros, worked at Athens, which was then the literary centre of Greece. Dionysius of Halicarnassos says that he was second to none as a genealogist. He certainly left no gaps in the record, and was particularly concerned to supply children, parents and names to people who previously had none. He named the six sons and six daughters of Niobe, who were killed by Apollo and Artemis, and the six men snatched by Scylla from Odysseus' ship. There was probably no mythological question that could not be answered by reference to Pherecydes. He knew how many ships Paris had taken with him for the abduction of Helen, and why Thersites was lame and misshapen: his uncle Meleager had damaged his head and foot by throwing him over a cliff because he would not take part in the fight over the Calydonian Boar.

Pherecydes appears to have touched modern history from above by means of heroic pedigrees, which he constructed for his contemporaries as Hecataios had done for himself. He is cited as the authority for the descent of the great physician Hippocrates of Cos in nineteen generations from Asclepios, and, as we have seen, for that of the first Miltiades in fourteen generations from Telamonian Aias. These myth-historians and genealogists certainly made the legends more accessible by publishing consistent versions in prose, but they complicated the stories with their imaginary relationships and ridiculous details, which were usually designed to contradict those of their predecessors. Pausanias complains, in trying to get at the true history of Rhadamanthos, that 'the legends of Greece differ from one another in most respects, and not least in the genealogies'.

The fifth century produced the first two historians in the modern sense, Herodotus and Thucydides, and the last two constructive mythographers, Pherecydes and Hellanicos. Hellanicos was said to have been born in the year 496, Herodotus in 484, and

Thucydides in 471, and all three lived until the last years of the century. The difference between the work of Acousilaos and Pherecydes and that of Herodotus and Thucydides was in method as well as subject-matter. Their books were all called *Histories* (Researches), but we should now distinguish them as ancient and modern history. The modern historians dealt with events contemporary with themselves or not far removed in time, though Herodotus was more discursive; they proceeded by enquiry, consideration of real evidence, and selective record. Acousilaos and Pherecydes wrote history in what Strabo calls the poetical manner: their research was compilation from the old epics and their method of enlargement was invention. There were indeed no other means of presenting ancient history, for the Greeks seem to have had no records, as distinct from lists of magistrates and unintelligibly dated decrees and treaties, before the fifth century. Thucydides says that events before the Peloponnesian War were forgotten in the lapse of time, and those of the prehistoric age had become incapable of proof and mythical.

Mythology as a general term comprises all imaginative accounts of supernatural and prehistoric persons and events, but myth is the usual name for the necessarily fictitious stories of religious origin, and is therefore appropriate to the equally fictitious systems of Greek ethnology. Legends are mythological stories which seem to have some historical content, however imaginative their characters and incidents may be. When Thucydides wrote that he proposed to omit the mythical element from his history, he meant something quite different from this. His myths were what we should call fables, incredible or irrelevant stories attached to historical personages.

All Greek historians accepted the legendary persons; those like Ephoros, who refused to write about them, did so because there was not enough authentic information to be had. Thucydides gives a circumstantial account of the legendary or mythical Amphilochos (page 94); adopts the Utopian Phaiacians of the *Odyssey* and identifies their island of Scheria with Corfù; accepts the *Cata-*

logue of Ships so thoroughly as to calculate from it the numbers of the Achaian force at Troy; and goes out of his way to explain that the mythical Tereus of Daulis, the central figure of the horrible and fantastic fairy-tale of Procnê and Philomela, was not in any way connected with the Teres who was a king of Thrace in his own time.

The survey of prehistoric Greece in the first book of Thucydides is a brilliant intellectual exercise composed by induction from assumed analogies and deduction from statements of the epics, but it is not history. His methods were sound but his basic materials were not. Archaeological and linguistic evidence and the testimony of foreign records were necessarily beyond his knowledge.

Hellanicos of Lesbos was the most prolific of the fifth-century authors, and wrote both ancient and modern history. He was particularly concerned with artificial chronology, as we have seen in his attempt to make a national canon with his *Priestesses of Hera*. That would have been a useful performance if he had not gone beyond the written register which must have existed for a century or two before him. But his inventive genius took him and the priestesses into unknown regions of time before the Dorian Invasion. We have seen that he dated a migration from Italy to Sicily in the twenty-sixth year of a priestess Alcyonê, three generations before the Trojan War, and the Fall of Troy in a certain year of a priestess Callisto. His mythical propensities are proclaimed by the titles of some of his books, which repeated those of the old epics, *Atlantis*, *Deucalionis*, *Phoronis*, and the like.

These myth-historians transcribed the legends from the epics, each publishing his own version, but they could not make major alterations because the old poets were always regarded as the authentic sources, so far as they were accessible, and Homer was the ultimate authority in matters which he had touched. But much could be done in tying up loose ends and filling gaps in pedigrees and incidents, an activity in which Hellanicos was prominent.

The trivialities in which these writers and their readers indulged are illustrated by the statement of a scholiast that Hellanicos said

Cadmos killed the Theban dragon with a sword, Pherecydes with a stone. Hellanicos also named the five men who sprang from the dragon's teeth. Another open question was, who made the rattle for Heracles? That was the instrument with which he scared the Stymphalian Birds in his Sixth Labour. Most authorities said that it was made by Hephaistos and given to Heracles by Athena, but Hellanicos said that he made it himself.

Hellanicos was congenially and perhaps profitably employed in providing Athenian nobles with heroic pedigrees. The orator Andocides was connected by him with Odysseus and Hermes through the marriage of Telemachos with Nausicaa; he seems to have collaborated with Pherecydes in the Orphic ancestry of Homer, and also in the Philaïd genealogy of Miltiades, since they are both cited as authorities for it. Thucydides belonged to the Philaïd clan, and it would be interesting to know if he accepted his own descent from Aias.

One geographical speculation of Hellanicos shows the ancient etymologist at his best. Dionysius reports him as saying that when Heracles was driving the cattle of Geryon from Spain, one of the calves 'skipped away' from the herd, ran down the length of Italy, and swam to Sicily. Heracles followed it, asking all the natives if anyone had seen his calf. He used the Greek word for it (*damalis*), which they did not understand; but they found out what he was after, translated its name into their own language (*vitulus*), and called all the country through which the calf had passed, *Witalia*.

Hellanicos has also the distinction of being the first Greek author who is known to have mentioned Rome. In reviewing discrepant accounts of its foundation, Dionysius says:

The writer who compiled the list of Priestesses at Argos, and the events that took place in the time of each, says that Aineias came to Italy from the Molossians with (or after) Odysseus, and became the founder of the city, naming it after one of the Trojan women, Romê. He says that this woman was tired of wandering, and incited the other Trojan women to join with her in setting fire to the ships. Damastes of Sigeion and some others agree with him.

This is a very different story from the one adopted by Virgil in the *Aeneid*. Aineias was taken to Molossis by Neoptolemos, either as a prisoner of war with Andromachê or with Helenos as a friendly Trojan. It cannot be supposed that any of these post-war fictions were based upon ancient legend or tradition.

The great Athenian dramatists of the fifth century, Aeschylus, Sophocles and Euripides, were exactly contemporary with Phere-cydes and Hellanicos. Between them and the end of the old epic there had been a century or more of elegiac and lyric poetry. Most of it was personal and topical, in revolt perhaps against the anony-mity and convention of the epic; but it retained the epic tradition in mythological allusions and short narratives, particularly in choral poetry, which is represented now by the odes of Pindar and Bacchylides and the musical interludes of Attic drama. The lyric poets do not seem to have altered or elaborated the legends, unless perhaps the famous Palinode of Stesichoros was the first enuncia-tion of the theory propounded by Herodotus, that Helen never went to Troy.

The story about Stesichoros was that he applied to Helen in an ode the epithets that Homer made her apply less forcibly to her-self. But the Helen of Stesichoros was a goddess, and blinded the poet for his irreverence. He recovered his eyesight by writing another ode, in which he retracted his previous censures, and ex-plained that Helen had spent the period of the war in Egypt, by contrivance of Zeus or Hera, who sent a replica of her to Troy. Plato quotes the opening lines of the *Palinode*:

> *That story is not true: thou didst not go*
> *Upon the oared ships nor to the towers of Troy.*

Herodotus repeats the tale (without what Thucydides would have called the mythical detail of the replica) as the Egyptian version of the incredible epic story of Helen's adventure, and the only reasonable explanation of Trojan behaviour in the war:

If Helen had been at Troy, the inhabitants would, I think, have given her up to the Greeks, whether Alexandros consented or not.

I do not believe that even if Priam had married her himself he would have refused to give her up.

It is often said that the dramatists took the subjects of their tragedies from heroic legend because the heroes were demigods and the drama was a religious performance. Aristotle says they need not have done so, but chose those plots because they were real: 'What is possible is credible, and what has happened is manifestly possible.' Athenian audiences demanded reality, but it must not be painful. There was a famous story of a topical tragedy produced by Phrynicos at the time of the Ionian revolt from Persia. It is told by Herodotus:

The Athenians showed in many ways their great distress at the destruction of Miletos, and when Phrynicos wrote and exhibited his *Capture of Miletos* the theatre burst into tears. They fined him a thousand drachmas for reminding them of a disaster which touched them closely, and decreed that the play should never be produced again.

That was the other side of the picture presented successfully by Aeschylus in his *Persians*.

Heroic tragedy was larger than life, operating among people who were real yet superhuman, and in immediate relations with divine powers which compelled or condoned their tragic behaviour. The gods were usually at hand to intervene, in Euripides by a comical device of stage machinery, when innocence came too close to irremediable injury. The material of the legends was in every sense ideal for comfortable contemplation of real but distant calamities.

The persons and incidents had been established by the epic, but there was ample room in tragedy for several poets, or indeed for the same poet, to present new aspects of behaviour and expression. Menelaos displays very different moral qualities, and the character and adventures of Helen are contradictory, in the *Orestes* and *Helena* of Euripides. In the latter play Euripides adopted the fantastic story told by Stesichoros, but when the poet diverged from the factual canon he was liable to be called to order by his commentators. On two lines in Euripides' *Andromachê*,

> Go thou and bury at the Pythian shrine
> This mortal body of Achilles' son,

a scholiast remarks 'That Neoptolemos was buried at Delphi agrees with what Pherecydes says, but that his body was taken to Phthia and sent back to Delphi is a falsification.' So Pausanias says of Oidipous: 'The account of his death in the tragedy of Sophocles I am prevented from believing by Homer, who says that after his death Mecisteos went to Thebes and took part in his funeral games.' It seems therefore that the dramatists added little to the legendary narratives, but brought the characters to life in novel and emotional scenes. Aristotle says that few people knew the stories previously.

The immense amount of legendary lore broadcast in the theatres and published by the lyric poets created a demand for mythological commentaries and handbooks, without which this classical literature could not be understood. They were also needed for use in schools. Later Greek poetry was largely a product of academic scholarship, and the learned and obscure allusions of such writers as Lycophron, Apollonius of Rhodes, Callimachus, their Alexandrian colleagues and Roman imitators, have provided inexhaustible material for pedantic study in all subsequent ages. Clement of Alexandria says that the *Aitia* and *Ibis* of Callimachus and the *Alexandra* of Lycophron (page 63) were set as exegetic exercises 'for the sons of the grammarians'.

The only Greek handbook of mythology that has survived is the *Bibliotheca* (Library) of Apollodorus. Its author was confused in late antiquity with the chronographer Apollodoros of Athens, who wrote in his second century B.C. (page 29); but the mention in his text of Castor, the successor of Apollodoros, puts the *Bibliotheca* at least a hundred years later, and certain grammatical peculiarities place it rather with Greek literature of the Roman Empire, in the first or second century A.D. The book covered the whole range of myth and legend, as the Epic Cycle had done, from the mating of Heaven and Earth, which produced the Titans and the gods, to the sons of the heroes who fought at Troy. About half of it exists in its original form; the substance of the rest is preserved in epitomes.

The mythography of Apollodorus differed from that of the logographers, with whom Acousilaos, Pherecydes and Hellanicos may be classed, in being neither critical nor inventive. It is a comprehensive record of myths and legends as they were represented in classical literature, without any suggestion that one version was more authentic or more plausible than another. It was an essential part of Apollodorus' scheme to note considerable variants: he usually quotes them with the phrase 'Some say' or 'Others say' or 'Many say'; but he often cites the authors who had invented or adopted them, not as authorities but as literary references.

Thus in his story of Io:

Argos and Ismenê had a son Iasos who is said to have been the father of Io. But Castor the chronographer and many of the tragedians say that Io was the daughter of Inachos, Hesiod and Acousilaos say she was the daughter of Peiren. Zeus seduced her while she was priestess of Hera, and when Hera found him out he turned the girl into a white cow by touching her, and swore he had not approached her: whereupon Hesiod says that perjury in love affairs does not incur the anger of the gods. Hera asked Zeus for the cow, and put all-seeing Argos in charge of it. Pherecydes says that this Argos was a son of Arestor, Asclepiades says of Inachos, Cercops says he was a son of Argos and Ismenê, Acousilaos says he was earth-born.

Acousilaos and Pherecydes were the secondary writers most frequently cited by Apollodorus, but he did not attach himself to either of them. His eclectic method was in fact a corrective of their positive assertions, and he often went beyond them to the primary sources, Homer, Hesiod, and the Cyclic poets.

It is a remarkable fact that although Apollodorus wrote when Greece and Asia were Imperial Roman provinces, he does not mention Rome. Its omission must have been deliberate, and can only be explained by the supposition that he refused to recognise the exploitation of Greek mythology by Etruscan and Roman foreigners. That process had begun long before his time and from the Greek side. Aineias and Odysseus had been taken to Rome, and Arcadians to Latium, in the fifth century; even Hesiod (or one of his interpolators) gave Odysseus and Circê a son Latinos. But Apollodorus would have none of these stories. He closed the canon of Greek mythology, so far as that may have any historical validity; but its later developments in Greece and Italy have considerable literary interest.

8

FICTION AND FACT

Epic and comedy – pre-Homeric imposture – Dictys of Crete – the magazines of Cnossos – 'Journal of the Trojan War' – Dares of Phrygia – Greek fiction – legend and history – plausibility and truth – 'The Song of Roland' – 'Nibelungenlied' – transference and combination – genealogy and chronology – tradition and invention.

The moral degradations of heroic legend, particularly those attached to the character of Achilles by late writers, need not be laid to the charge of Rome or Byzantium. The tragic hero was ready-made material for mock-heroic comedy, and the gods themselves were legitimately travestied on the Greek stage. Odysseus and Diomedes, Achilles and Patroclos, Orestes and Pylades, were soon turned into boon companions and figures of fun, and theatrical fun was hardly separable from scurrility. Comic and satyric drama also offered privileged indulgence in religious scepticism which could not be safely expressed in ordinary life or literature. Homer's ignoble deities were reformed by the philosophers, his noble heroes were reduced to absurdity by the comedians.

Transition from tragedy to comedy was natural and easy, but the desire to discredit Homer himself seems to be less reasonable. The process may have begun with exaggerated appreciation of his merits and the desire to provide him with a mythical ancestry.

Many poets were popularly named as predecessors of Homer, putative inventors of hexameter verse or authors of current ritual hymns. Some were mythical, as Oiagros, Linos, Orpheus and Mousaios, others were poetical fictions, as Phemios and Demodocos, the two minstrels attached in the *Odyssey* to the palaces of Odysseus and Alcinoös. Homer was of course related to some of these: he was a son of Phemios or a descendant of Orpheus in the eleventh generation. The judgment passed by Herodotus upon the works attributed to these imaginary authors was generally accepted in course of time: 'As for the poets who are thought by some to be earlier than Homer and Hesiod, they are in my opinion decidedly later writers.'

Oiagros was said to have been the first Greek poet of the Trojan War, but those who sought Hellenic origins in Egypt attributed the *Iliad* and *Odyssey* to a poetess of Memphis appropriately named Phantasia. Homer was said to have obtained copies of them from one Phanites, a temple scribe. Several pretenders to better authority than Homer's were more precisely designated, and equipped with documentary credentials.

Suidas reports that Corinnos of Troy was thought by some to have written the *Iliad* during the war, in the 'Dorian script' which Palamedes had invented and taught him, and that Homer took the whole substance of his poems from this. One Sisyphos of Cos was said to have been a combatant on the Greek side, a friend of Teucros the brother of Aias. The Byzantine chronicler John Malalas reports that Sisyphos wrote the history of the war on first-hand authority, that Homer found it and produced some in the *Iliad*, and Virgil the rest. An independent witness on the Trojan side was Dares of Phrygia. Both these reputed authors had books attributed to them which have survived to some extent in late Greek or Latin versions. A more effective impostor wrote under the name of Dictys of Crete, and professed to be a companion of Idomeneus. His *Journal of the Trojan War* exists in a Latin translation; the original Greek text is represented on a single fragment of papyrus found in Egypt.

These books are amusing examples of the device of the ancient document, first attributed to Acousilaos in the sixth century B.C. (page 142). Its use by the unknown author who posed as the editor of Dictys was particularly ingenious, as may be seen in his preface, to which topical interest has been restored by recent archaological discovery:

Dictys was Cretan by birth, a citizen of Cnossos, and was versed in the Phoenician language and script which Cadmos had introduced into Achaia. He was a companion of Idomeneus son of Deucalion and Meriones son of Molos, who were military commanders in the expedition against Ilion and instructed Dictys to write a chronicle of the war. He therefore recorded the whole war in nine volumes written in Phoenician characters on strips of bark, and returning to Crete in his later years he gave instructions at his death that these should be buried with him. So the leaves were enclosed in a tin box and hidden in his grave.

In later times, in the thirteenth year of the reign of Nero, an earthquake which occurred at Cnossos opened many tombs, among them that of Dictys in such a way that the box was exposed to view. Thus it was seen by shepherds passing by, who took it from the tomb thinking it was treasure. When they opened it and found bark inscribed with strange writing, they took it immediately to their master, by name Eupraxis, who recognised what they were and submitted the documents to Rutilius Rufus, the governor of the island at that time. He sent them with Eupraxis himself to Nero, thinking that they contained secret information.

When Nero received them and saw that the writing was Phoenician, he summoned experts in that language, who came and interpreted all the documents. Finding that they were records of an ancient man who had been at Ilion, Nero directed that they should be translated into Greek, so that a more authentic narrative of the Trojan War has become generally known from them. He dismissed Eupraxis with material rewards and Roman citizenship, and deposited in his Greek library the chronicle inscribed with the name of Dictys, of which the content is exhibited in the following text.

Among the first discoveries made by Arthur Evans at Cnossos, when he began his excavation of the palace, was a long series of narrow basement-rooms behind the outer wall of the west front. Many of these still contain their original storage-jars, and have small cists sunk in their stone-paved floors, which seem to have held valuable commodities. Some of the cists held remains of lead linings, and in the filling of the magazines were large numbers of inscribed clay tablets which had fallen from rooms above. These are the 'strips of bark' of Dictys, the lead-lined cists explain the 'tin box', and the magazines themselves look very much like tombs (Plate 8).

Earthquakes have always been a frequent reality at Cnossos, and there may have been a notoriously destructive one in the time of Nero. But no earthquake could have had the effect of clearing a magazine, nor was that needed to reveal the contents. Many walls of the palace stood above ground in Roman times, inviting investigation, and the magazines would have been a productive hunting-ground for treasure. A similar Minoan site at Mallia in Crete is still called the Pit of Gold (*Chrysolakkos*). The thin clay tablets of Cnossos (Plate 8) must have been well known as a local curiosity, though they could not be recognised as native documents. We have already examined historical Greek knowledge of the prehistoric scripts. But the author of the preface to the Latin translation of Dictys brings the original fiction nearer to fact than he knew, by saying that the language of the documents was Greek and the text had merely to be transliterated from the Phoenician to the Attic alphabet. The papyrus manuscript is assigned to the third century A.D. The Greek author must therefore have written between that time and the reign of Nero, but his references to the Emperor's part in the matter suggest that the imposture was well removed from the alleged events.

The narrative of Dictys (as we must call the author) does not differ to any considerable extent from the Cyclic catalogue of events, so far as that is known to us, or from the description of the Fall of Troy that Virgil attributes to Aineias. But Dictys pretends to personal knowledge of what went on behind the scenes, and assigns motives for the behaviour of individuals. His Latin translation reads like the work of an Imperial historian recording a frontier campaign with its attendant political and strategical problems and considerations of commissariat and discipline.

The Trojan people were disaffected from the first, and were supported by many of the nobles against Priam and his sons.

Greek loyalties were strained by personal rivalries among the leaders. Palamedes displaced Agamemnon as commander-in-chief until Odysseus and Diomedes disposed of him by dropping stones on his head in a well, into which he had unwisely descended in search of hidden treasure. Military rationalism is a novel element, and sentimental love-interest, particularly associated with the moral and physical destruction of Achilles, is another. Helen falls in love with Paris and out of love with Menelaos: she explains to the Trojan Council that she left Greece willingly, because the Pelopid marriage was distasteful to her.

Greeks and Trojans used to meet amicably in time of truce or holiday at a temple of Thymbraian Apollo near the city. Achilles saw Polyxena, Priam's youngest daughter, on one of those occasions, loved her at first sight and offered to betray the Greek army in return for her hand in marriage. But Paris took the opportunity to stab him at their final conference in the temple, and by that act of sacrilege lost what support he had in Troy.

The capture of the city was accompanied by treachery on both sides. The Trojans agreed to pay a war indemnity, two thousand talents each of gold and silver, which the Greeks received and ostensibly sailed for home. But they sailed back at night, Aineias and Antenor opened the gates as prearranged, and the city was sacked as if it had been taken by assault.

The *History of the Fall of Troy* claimed for Dares of Phrygia exists in a Latin prose version which seems to have been written about the sixth century A.D., but may be an abridgment of an earlier Greek or Latin original. It is introduced by a spurious letter purporting to be written by Cornelius Nepos, the Augustan biographer, to his friend Sallustius Crispus:

In the course of my researches at Athens I found a history written by the hand of Dares of Phrygia, in which, as its title indicates, he commemorated the deeds of Greeks and Trojans. I seized upon it eagerly and translated it forthwith. I did not think that anything ought to be taken from it or added to it by way of improvement, considering too that this might seem to be my doing; but I thought

it best to turn its true and simple narrative literally into Latin, so
that readers may know what really happened: whether they think
there is more truth in the record of Dares of Phrygia, who lived
and served in the army when the Greeks defeated the Trojans, or
would rather believe Homer, who was born many years after the
war was fought. In which question judgment was passed at
Athens, when Homer was condemned as a lunatic for saying that
gods fought with men.

The *History* of Dares, like the *Journal* of Dictys, is no more than
a literary curiosity, and its text is less interesting than the letter. It
is a bare summary of events similar to those described by Dictys,
but sufficiently varied in sequence and detail to support its claim to
independent authorship. There is even more insistence upon the
supremacy of Palamedes, but he comes to a different end, being
shot by Paris in an archery duel. There is the same treachery on
both sides, and the same infatuation of Achilles with Polyxena,
leading to his murder in the temple and her slaughter at his tomb.
The only new ideas in Dares are additions to the unlikely realism
with which all mythographers and historians had tried to redeem
the ancient legends. He accounts for the paucity of incidents in the
nine-years siege by interpolating continual truces, extending from
days or months to two and three years, during which the combatants heal their wounds and renew supplies. His realism rises to supreme absurdity in a portrait-gallery of leading characters on both
sides:

Helen was as handsome as her fair-haired brothers, simple-minded,
charming, with very fine legs, a mole between her eyebrows, and
a tiny mouth. Nestor was tall, broad, fair, with a long hooked
nose,

and so on. These last contributions to the ancient Tale of Troy
have at least the unintentional merit of being manifestly false. Even
so, Dictys and Dares were the authorities who transmitted the tale
to medieval historians in Western Europe.

Classical Greek fiction produced as such did not attempt to
represent fact; if it had done so, it would have been condemned

as falsehood. It was accepted on low or modest levels where it could not seriously be mistaken for truth, as in animal fables (associated with the name of Aesop), amusing and rather scurrilous anecdotes (later published as Milesian Tales), and parodies of every-day life, as the *Margites* which Aristotle and others attributed to Homer. He might have added the Homeric *Battle of the Frogs and Mice*, but may have thought it beneath his notice and beneath the dignity of Homer. Less incredible fables and fairy-tales were attracted to the service of history and attached to real persons, as the dancing peacock at Agaristê's wooing, and the sunbeam embraced by the youngest brother in the pedigree of the Macedonian kings.

Obvious fiction was continued in mimes and comedies, in which the characters had no actuality, unless they were caricatures of living persons. The characters of tragedy, and what Aristotle calls the nobler poetry, were known heroic persons whose existence was not doubted. Attic dramas were in fact historical novels in poetical form.

Aristotle has in his *Poetics* an illuminating description of the process by which he thought they ought to be constructed:

You must lay out a general scheme of the story, whether it is ready-made or you make it yourself. Then you divide it into episodes and elaborate it like this: I mean, for instance, one might consider the general scheme of the *Iphigeneia*. Some girl is sacrificed and disappears beyond the knowledge of the people who sacrificed her, etc. [Here he outlines the plot of *Iphigeneia in Tauris*.] Only when this is done do you put in the names and arrange the episodes. But you must get your episodes right, for instance the madness of Orestes that led to his capture, and his deliverance through the purification (of the image).

This was all very well in theory, but in fact the dramatists were tied to the epic stories as much as to the epic names. Classical Greek authors and their Roman imitators had little opportunity for original narrative, and no idea of its potentialities. Aristotle calls Euripides the most tragic of the tragedians: we should say that his plays represent the nearest ancient approach to the modern novel, but his studies of mentality and behaviour were necessarily confined to a few legendary persons whose characters and actions were for the most part fixed.

Religious myth was wholly fictitious, though its growth may have been unconscious; that is to say, it was the work of many generations of men and in that sense was traditional. The oral epos is likely to have been similarly formed upon a core of fact. Literary fiction began with Homer and ended with the Cyclic poets. Most of the Asiatic personages in the *Iliad* must be fictitious, since they could not have belonged to an original Achaian legend. Some, as Bellerophon and Sarpedon, were demonstrably transferred from religious myth, and their exploits were as imaginary as those of Memnon and the Amazons, Palamedes, Neoptolemos, and other unreal characters in the Cyclic sequels.

The most considerable piece of fiction in the *Iliad* is the tenth book, the midnight reconnaissance of Diomedes and Odysseus leading to their capture of the Trojan spy, Dolon, and their slaughter of the Thracian Rhesos. It is a brilliantly presented story, though apparently by a later poet than the rest of the *Iliad*. The author's circumstantial detail is as convincing as anything that Homer wrote, and he too did not try to disguise his inventions. Rhesos was probably a legendary Thracian prince with no more historical reality than Memnon, but the central figure, Dolon, after whom the book was named (*Doloneia*), is shown to be fictitious by his own name and his father's, Eumedes: 'Wily son of Artful'. After this introduction the poet is particularly realistic about the man: 'He was a lordly herald's son, rich in gold, rich in bronze; ugly to look at but swift of foot. He was the only brother among five sisters.'

The *Odyssey* is a masterpiece of fiction, an enthralling fantasy of adventure and romance, real life and fairy-tale, lightly attached to the war of Troy. Homer evidently meant his creations to be enjoyed as works of art. He presents the Phaiacians as human but imaginary beings, and says explicitly that their island of Scheria is

not of this world, but is 'far from men who live by toil, and no
other mortals are in touch with them'. Their behaviour was en-
tirely realistic, but most of their names were openly fictitious, being compounded from ships and shipping, as befitted people who
were wizards of the sea. Yet Thucydides, representing the higher
criticism of his day, placed the Phaiacians in Corfù.

It is easier to understand why these intellectual Greeks rejected
fiction in principle than why in practice they accepted so much
obvious fiction as historical fact. The main reason seems to be that
when they first turned their attention to historical literature in the
sixth century, they recognised that they possessed no ancient
records comparable with the inscribed and written documents of
Egypt and Asia, an inferiority of which they were uncomfortably
reminded by their neighbours in those countries, as by the aged
Egyptian priest in his talk with Solon, reported by Plato in the
Timaeus, or more forcibly by Josephus in his *Reply to Apion*. Since
the epic legends at least resembled history, and also had the sanction of religious and poetical tradition, they were established as a
whole and beyond question. As history they were also beyond enlargement. Major characters could not be added, nor could heroic
adventures be extended in time or space. Poetic genius was guided
by the same limitations to a higher destiny than the invention
of narrative, but the prose mythographers were condemned to
endless repetition and detail.

Many reasons might be found for the general failure to appre-
ciate fiction on these higher levels: one was certainly the philosophical reverence for truth as an ideal virtue, another the actual fear
of being deceived, the latter being the weightier with those who
had no philosophy. Inveterate suspicion does not seem to have
been a natural defect of the Hellenic character, but was due to in-
security of private life in the city state. Its effect was the practice
of deceit as a defensive art. Pindar praises the man who can mis-
lead his enemy by crooked ways, and the tyrant Hipparchos was
said to have posted in the streets of Athens, among other civic pre-
cepts, 'Do not deceive a friend.' To believe a story that was not

true would have been the last infirmity of Hellenic intelligence.

It was apparently the philosophic view that Solon was said to have expressed in the first recorded dramatic criticism. The story is told by Plutarch in his *Life of Solon*:

When the company of Thespis began to exhibit tragedy, and its novelty was attracting the populace but had not yet got as far as public competitions, Solon, being fond of listening and learning and being rather given in his old age to leisure and amusement, and indeed to drinking-parties and music, went to see Thespis act in his own play, as was the practice in ancient times. Solon approached him after the performance and asked him if he was not ashamed to tell so many lies to so many people. When Thespis said there was nothing dreadful in representing such words and actions in fun, Solon struck the ground violently with his walking-stick: 'If we applaud these things in fun,' he said, 'we shall soon find ourselves honouring them in earnest.'

The old epic poets, who had no philosophical or historical critics, did not suffer from these inhibitions. They and their audiences were interested only in the stories, and the actions of gods and demigods transcended the realities of life. Homer at least was plausible on human levels, but his Cyclic successors were less careful in that respect, and the logographers, while professing to reform them, seem rather to have enjoyed the licence offered by their example. On that ground alone the poets and myth-historians were ultimately discredited, as by Strabo in reviewing some of his predecessors who had written on Oriental history: 'One could more easily believe Homer and Hesiod or the tragic poets in their heroic tales than Ctesias, Herodotus, Hellanicos, and others of their kind.' It is strange to find Herodotus in this company. He certainly told many incredible tales about Egypt and the East, but was careful to explain that he considered it his duty to report what he had heard, without vouching for the truth of it.

These later criticisms were not directed against the legends themselves but against the manner in which they had been presented. When the improbable incidents (the 'myths' of Thucydides) were removed, the persons and their transactions were accepted as historical.

Reliance upon plausibility as a measure of truth is an obvious fallacy, but it is often used, without the ancient justification for it, in modern evaluation of the legends. These were the only ancient history that the Greeks possessed, and they were also religious testimonies, like the biblical traditions of the Hebrews and the Christian lives of saints which were devoutly believed in the Middle Ages. Plausible fiction can only be distinguished from fact by external evidence, which was not available to Greek historians. They had no prehistoric documents, no comparative material, no archaeological experience and no access to foreign records.

The historical content of any particular legend must finally be established by historical knowledge, which is not yet available for the Greek Heroic Age. Archaeological discovery may determine times and places of certain events, but the peoples or persons properly associated with them can only be identified by contemporary written records. Progress may be made, in the absence of such historical information, by eliminating obvious fictions and by considering other processes by which legend tends to be distorted or falsified. Some of these are represented in epic poems which celebrate known historical events.

The French *Song of Roland* professes to record a great Frankish battle with Saracens at the pass of Roncevaux in the Pyrenees, when Charlemagne was returning from Spain at the end of a seven-years war. Roland and his companion Oliver are in command of the rearguard, which is cut up in a treacherous attack. They die heroically, Charlemagne is recalled at the last moment and defeats the Saracen host, which is reinforced by an army brought from Egypt by the Emir of Babylon (Cairo).

The facts recorded in the Frankish annals and by the Abbot Eginhard (Einhart) in his *Life of Charles the Great* (written a few years after the events) are that in the year 778 Charlemagne led an expedition into Spain, at the request of the Moorish Emir of Saragossa, and captured several Christian towns. On the return march his rearguard was attacked at Roncevaux by the Basques of Pampeluna: 'Eggihard, master of the king's table, Anselm, count of the palace, and Hruodtland, commander of the Breton march, were killed with many others.' Charlemagne took no part in the affair (unless as Gibbon suggests, by bad generalship), and fought no war with Saracens. On the contrary, he was on good terms with them, being in friendly correspondence with the Khalif, Haroun al Raschid, at Baghdad, and having invaded Spain in alliance with a Moorish prince.

In this instance the name of one hero and his association with Charlemagne and Roncevaux have been preserved correctly by the poets, but the enemy is totally misrepresented, the seven-years war, the great battle, and the final victory, are imaginary, the Moorish champions fictitious, and many of the Frankish characters, as Ganelon the traitor, were personages of later French history. The fabulous expedition of the Emir of Egypt, which is curiously like that of Memnon at the siege of Troy, must have been derived from experiences of the first Crusades. The *Song of Roland* in its final form belongs to the twelfth century or thereabouts.

Another medieval legend which can be examined in the light of history is that of Sigurd and Gudrun (Siegfried and Kriemhild) in its Norse, and South German, versions. The hero and heroine, whoever they may have been, are associated with a Burgundian king Gunnar (Gunther). He is evidently the person known in contemporary history as Gundicarius, whose kingdom was broken up by the Roman Aetius in the year 435. In the last episodes of the *Nibelungenlied* Attila the Hun (Etzel) and Theodoric the Ostrogoth 'of Verona' (Dietrich von Berne) are introduced into the action, Etzel as the second husband of Kriemhild, Gunther's sister, Dietrich as a visitor in Etzel's palace. Attila and Gundicarius were partly contemporaneous, but there is no reason to believe that they had personal contacts by marriage or otherwise. The last of Attila's many brides, Ildico, in whose bed he died, was certainly not a sister of Gundicarius. Theodoric was born in or about the year of Attila's death, 453 A.D. These tendencies of famous events to be exaggerated in importance, to be combined with earlier and later events of the same kind, and to attract the participation of famous persons who lived at different times or places, must be suspected in all heroic legend.

The only Greek epics of which we have even a general account are those of the Trojan war. The *Iliad*, being the earliest of them, ought to stand nearest to historical truth, but we have seen that many of its persons and episodes were fictitious. Historical considerations support the probability suggested by poetical analogies that the circumstances of the war were greatly exaggerated in the epic. The numbers and organisation of the Achaian force, as represented in the *Catalogue of Ships*, and the long siege of the city, are unlikely. Nine was a conventional number for great efforts, as Minos in the *Odyssey* is a nine-year king and Odysseus swims for nine days and nights after his shipwreck. It is also reasonable to suppose that all the Achaian heroes of the *Iliad* were not contemporary with one another, even if they were real. The fictitious persons of Homer are usually minor characters; others may have been figures of religious myth or folk-lore, as Iphigeneia and Palamedes have been shown to be in the Cyclic poems. But it is likely, since Achaian Greece was isolated, as the countries of medieval Europe were not, that external contamination of the legend has operated only on the Trojan side, with such characters as Rhesos, Memnon, and the Lycian and Mysian kings, and at a late moment, after the colonial migrations to Asia.

Fictional narrative was fully elaborated in the old epic, and came to an end with the beginning of prose literature, when the legends were caught up in the net of history. But inventive ingenuity, imitating the methods of historical record, found a new occupation in devising genealogical and ethnographical relationships for epic personages. We have seen that Homer, and presumably the earlier epos, had little interest in genealogy beyond the actual parentage of heroes. Even so, if Homer had known the fact or tradition that Achilles and Aias were first cousins, he would surely have referred to it in the long course of the *Iliad*, where

these two are the foremost Achaian champions. He had more than
an opportunity to do so when Aias was one of the three delegates
chosen to persuade Achilles to forgo his wrath, and they made
their appeal on personal as well as public grounds. Achilles in
Homer is usually Peleiades (son of Peleus), often Aiacides (grandson of Aiacos); Aias is Telamonios or 'son of Telamon', never
Aiacides. Yet Telamon in the later legend was a son of Aiacos and
brother of Peleus.

The double Aiacid pedigree was the most imposing product of
the genealogists, being brought down to reality on one side
(Achilles) in the persons of Epeirote and Macedonian kings, on
the other (Aias) in Athenian aristocrats of the Philaïd clan. Aiacos
himself was a mythical personage, a son of Zeus and Aigina,
daughter of the river Asôpos. Zeus settled mother and son in the
island of Aigina and peopled it with ants (*myrmêkes*) turned into
men: they were the Myrmidones whom Peleus took away to
Thessaly and Achilles took to Troy. Telamon left Aigina for
Salamis, where Aias was born and where his pretended son or
grandson, Philaios, was planted by the Athenians when they
annexed the island in the sixth century.

Aias was doubtless at home in Salamis, either as a hero or a local
deity, and seems to have been associated with Aiacos through the
resemblance of their names, as he was with the Athenian family
eponym Philaios. Hesiod said that Aias was so named because his
birth was presaged by an eagle (*aietos*). The common pedigree
must have been a very late invention. Even the Hesiodic con-
tinuator of the *Theogony* did not make Telamon a son of Aiacos,
and Apollodorus quotes Pherecydes as affirming that Peleus and
Telamon were not brothers but only friends, Telamon being a son
of Actaios the first king of Attica. All this was political propaganda
supported by etymological nonsense and had no historical reality,
but it illustrates materials and methods used by the genealogists in
their enlargements of the legends.

Artificial relationships, invented by Hesiodic poets and improved by Acousilaos and his successors, were the basis of the

chronological structures built up by Hellanicos and others and represented in the prehistoric annals of the Parian Marble. These were no more traditional than the material fictions, inscribed and dedicated in temples of the gods, which we perhaps too hastily condemn as forgeries. The historical traditions, which had been more or less accurately preserved by the oral epos, must have been incorporated in the literary epic, where they were overlaid, as we see even in the *Iliad*, with so much conscious and unconscious fiction and combined with so many alien elements that the original facts cannot be recovered by any critical analysis. Archaeological discovery may throw light upon the legends, but the use of legendary statements for historical interpretation of material records is a reversal of proper procedure. It is not far removed from the ancient practice of constructing archaeological documents to fit the legends, and reproduces the credulity without the piety of the Lindian and Theban priests.

APPENDIX

Hippias, *sophist* B.C. 420
Homer, *epic poet* B.C. 820?
Jerome, *theologian* A.D. 380
Josephus, *historian* A.D. 70
Lesches, *epic poet* B.C. 650?
Lycophron, *dramatic poet*
B.C. 280
Lysias, *orator* B.C. 420
Malalas, *historian* A.D. 580
Marcellinus, *biographer*
c. A.D. 400
Panyassis, *epic poet* B.C. 480
Pausanias, *antiquary* A.D. 140
Pherecydes, *mythographer*
B.C. 460
Photius, *Patriarch* A.D. 850
Phrynichos, *tragic poet* B.C. 490
Pindar, *choral poet* B.C. 480

Plato, *philosopher* B.C. 390
Plutarch, *biographer* A.D. 80
Polybius, *historian* B.C. 160
Proclos, *philosopher* A.D. 450
Sophocles, *tragic poet* B.C. 450
Sosibios, *historian* B.C. 250
Stasinos, *epic poet* B.C. 650?
Stesichoros, *lyric poet c.* B.C. 580
Strabo, *geographer* B.C. 20
Suidas, *lexicographer* A.D. 1000?
Syncellus, *chronographer* A.D. 800
Theopompos, *historian* B.C. 340
Thespis, *tragic poet* B.C. 540
Thucydides, *historian* B.C. 430
Timaios, *historian* B.C. 270
Tzetzes, *grammarian* A.D. 1150
Xenophanes, *philosopher* B.C. 530
Xenophon, *historian* B.C. 400

INDEX